Francis Sinclair

Ballads and Poems from the Pacific

Francis Sinclair

Ballads and Poems from the Pacific

ISBN/EAN: 9783744775571

Printed in Europe, USA, Canada, Australia, Japan

Cover: Foto ©Thomas Meinert / pixelio.de

More available books at **www.hansebooks.com**

BALLADS AND POEMS

FROM THE PACIFIC.

BY

PHILIP GARTH,

("F. S. C.," "AOPOURI").

"In ye farre londs ayont ye mone and sunne—
Fayre londs o' wondrous thynges—
Whaur tyme's drade scythe is ydle, sand-glas runne,
And sweete luve faulds hys wynges."

OLD BALLAD.

London:
SAMPSON LOW, MARSTON, SEARLE, & RIVINGTON,
CROWN BUILDINGS, 188, FLEET STREET.
1885.

[*All rights reserved.*]

CONTENTS.

	PAGE
PROEM	1
GREETING	5
THE PHANTOM SHIP	9
A SKETCH IN THE PACIFIC	16
CAPTAIN TEACH	30
THE WHALER "DEVONPORT"	41
WITH FRANKY DRAKE	54
ISANDLANA	61
IN MEMORIAM—PRINCE IMPERIAL	64
FOUNDERED IN THE JAVA SEA	67
THE SPANISH CAPTAIN	70
CLOTHO	77
CHANGE	80
MY SHIP	84

	PAGE
THE ROLL CALL	88
DRIFTING APART	93
THE LOTUS	96
ELUIA	99
GHOSTS	102
THE OLD LOVE	105
DEAD	109
WAITING	112
IN MEMORIAM—GARIBALDI	116
THE DROWNED MAIDEN	119
GIVE BACK	122
THE HOUSE WE BUILD AT LAST	124
"VANITY OF VANITIES"	127
AKANBAR	130
IN THE GULF OF DULCÉ	147
THE DYING BUSHRANGER	154
THE AFGHAN'S VERSION OF THE CAMPAIGN, 1840—1842	159
ISLES OF THE BLEST	163
THERE IS A ROAD THAT WE MUST TREAD	166
THE SHIPS	169

CONTENTS.

	PAGE
LINES UPON HEARING A BLIND GIRL PLAY "HOME, SWEET HOME"	172
THE DYING CHIEF	175
THE SADDEST THING	180
OH, TRAVELLER OUT IN THE NIGHT	183
"AS MANY AS I LOVE, I REBUKE AND CHASTEN"	187
TREASURES OF THE DEEP	189
A FRAGMENT	193
A VOICE FROM THE SEA	196
BROTHERHOOD	200
THE BURIAL OF THE EARL	203
THE CONFESSION	205
"THE BURDEN OF THE DESERT OF THE SEA"	219
THE SPECTRE HORSEMAN	224
WHAT IS LIFE?	235
THE DIFFERENCE BETWEEN A WISE MAN AND A FOOL	241
YARROW BRAES	244
THE HEATHER	248
ELLEN O' ANGUS	250
OUR KNIGHT IS DEAD	255
THE NIGHTINGALES	259

PROEM.

I.

THESE are the voices heard so faint and lightly,

That their music and their rhythm are fled,

Uttered by magic lips that charm me nightly,

But when the sad day dawns are cold and dead!

II

Ah! if the tender beauty and the sweetness,

Of all the unsung songs within my heart;

(The beauty of the rainbow, with its fleetness),

Could be uttered wholly, not in part!

III.

Then, my songs, instead of feeble meaning,

(As of whispers heard in ocean shells

Of the sea, half real and half dreaming),

Would hold and charm you, waking with their spells.

IV.

And in sleep, their mystery and their sadness,

Would linger like the sound of far-off seas ;

Like skylark's early summer song of gladness ;

Like the wail of winter wind through leafless trees.

V.

But my heart, and not my lips, received the chrism

Of the mystic touch of fire, and tender song ;

And though my soul can read the wondrous prism,

Which the angels hold to mortals all life long—

VI.

Yet my lips are slow, and cold, and cannot render

Into speech the lavish gifts of wondrous things;

Of songs as pure, and high, and sweet, and tender,

As the grand majestic sweep of angels' wings!

VII.

I have gathered, here and there on faeric islands,

Such flowers as my rude feeble hands could reach;

I have climbed grief's cloud-enveloped highlands,

And brought back a whisper of their mournful speech.

VIII.

But the heights beyond the clouds I may not enter;

I can only stand and listen from afar

To the roll of rhythm from utmost verge to centre,

To the music of the spheres from star to star.

IX.

Yet perchance some wanderer mute with sorrows,

With life's shadows gathering thick and fast

O'er all the lost ! lost ! years, and hopeless morrows,

May hear and know a brother's voice at last !

X.

If so ! if one sad heart is made the lighter ;

One wounded soul forgets one hour its pain ;

If one dark path by me is made the brighter,

Ah ! then my lowly songs are not in vain.

GREETING.

Oh, England! mother England! I have wandered far and long,
Where the southern seas are laving the Hesperides of song;
Where the cross of stars is gleaming over wondrous isles of palm,
Where rose-hued reefs of coral flash through seas of perfect calm.

I have lived the dream of mystics—where eternal summer smiles—
Floating over seas of purple by the far, enchanted isles;

Where the seething haste of Europe—rushing deed—and jarring speech—

And the restless march of ages—cruel ages ! may not reach.

Where the dreamy days drift slowly into vaults of amber light,

Filled with rapturous gales of odour, shaken by the hand of night,

From bowers that bend and shimmer 'neath their wealth of fruit and flowers,

Where the gay cicada trills his song through all night's charmèd hours.

Where the curse of labour comes not, where earth's gifts are full and free—

Lavish gifts of generous nature, yielded up by land and sea ;

GREETING.

Where is heard no moan of sorrow, and where sad tears
    never fall,
Where the dreams of youth ne'er vanish, and where love
    reigns queen of all.

But oh, England, mother England! I return to thy dear
    breast,
For thy love is more than dreaming, and thy life is more
    than rest;
Every hallowed memory clinging to thy hedgerows,
    mountains, streams,
Holds a spell o'er all thy children, stronger far than
    wayward dreams.

Take me to thy bosom, mother! I thy prodigal returned
To thy altar fires of freedom, that a thousand years have
    burned;

Higher far I hold my birthright, and the name my fathers bore,

Than all magic dreams of beauty from earth's furthest shore to shore.

THE PHANTOM SHIP.

BEYOND that cape where skies are never bright,
  Shrouded in mist and gloom,
Where icebergs heave and moan by day and night,
  There sails a ship till doom.

Her sails are never lowered or anchor cast,
  No rest may that ship know;
Her doom was sealed, her day of grace went past
  Two hundred years ago.

Her sails are sere and thin, and sailors tell,
  When storms are wild and high
(Warning of coming ill, an omen fell),
  The phantom ship goes by.

Two hundred years ago that ship unfurled
  And shook her white sails down ;
While in the morning sun the blue smoke curled
  Above the old Dutch town.

Familiar sounds came floating softly out
  Across the pleasant bay ;
Familiar sounds of life, the laugh and shout
  Of children at their play.

The sailors, heaving at the anchor, sang
  A merry, rough sea rhyme ;
The bell within the quaint old chapel rang
  A sweet, sad parting chime.

The bearded captain by the helmsman stood,
  And proudly conned his ship ;
And cursed his sailors, as in angry mood,
  To hide his quivering lip.

THE PHANTOM SHIP.

For by the gate his little daughter stands,

   The sunlight in her hair;

And waves to him her little dimpled hands;

   Her mother waves a prayer.

Ah me! ah me! was evil in the air

   From him whom mortals fear,

Turning aside the tears, and wail and prayer,

   That Jesu might not hear?

The harbour bar was passed; the pilot's shout

   Was answered yet again;

And then the brave good ship stood boldly out

   Into the boundless main.

And day by day, they ever southward sped,

   With merry flowing sheet,

Taking no thought of all the silent dead,

   Who slept beneath their feet.

Earth's central line was passed; the southern cape
   Rose bleak and tempest scarred;
The storm lights gathered, and assumed a shape,
   And clung to mast and yard!

The icebergs, from earth's utmost verge came out,
   Stalking across the waves,
Scattering the wild sea foam that howled about
   Their terror-haunted caves.

The white snow whirled and danced, the glancing sleet,—
   Borne on the angry blast—
Rattled on creaking yard and straining sheet,
   Wet sail and bending mast.

Unceasingly the cruel tempest blew,
   No rest—no peaceful rest!—
Came to the labouring ship and weary crew,
   Fighting towards the west.

And so by day and night, by day and night,

   Stout ship and stouter men,

Fought with the storm and fate, as brave men fight

   A hopeless fight; and then

Spake an old sailor, in all omens wise,

   "Oh, captain, do not spurn

These warnings of the sea and air and skies,

   Take thought! take thought! and turn."

A fiend came gliding through the mist and spray,

   Working his evil spell;

(Oh, child and mother, wake! oh, wake and pray

   For him you love so well.)

"I will not turn," quoth he, and stamped his feet,

   With fierce and angry e'e,—

"My ship shall sail, till heaven and hell shall meet,

   Ere I will turn and flee!"

Through the wild tempest, far above the din,
    The fiend laughed loud and high,
"The fight is o'er, hurrah ! I win, I win !
    Oh, king, whom I defy !"

And through the storm-wrack, plainer, plainer heard,
    Weirdly a child's wail rings ;
High on the giddy mast, a snow-white bird
    Folded her trembling wings.

A sunbeam, for a moment darting through,
    Glittered, and glanced, and shone—
On bird or spirit ! fated ship and crew,
    A moment, and was gone !

Like spreading arms, the cloud-rack overhead,
    Gathered in sullen gloom ;
And in its fold hid ship and living-dead,
    To dree their weary doom !

To dree their weary doom! And sailors tell,

When storms are wild and high

(Warning of coming ill, an omen fell),

The phantom ship goes by.

A SKETCH IN THE PACIFIC.

I.

IN my youth's summer, when my hopes were high,
 It chanced my wandering steps did lead me where
The broad Pacific rolls beneath a sky
 Blue as itself;—where all is soft and fair;
Where fairy isles of wondrous beauty lie,
 Loading with lotos breath the charmèd air;
Where the soft day gives place to softer night,
And all things seem but formed to give delight.

II.

And one there was—a land beyond compare,
　Sweeter than dreaming eye had ever seen;
More softly tinted, delicately fair
　Than fabled islands of the blest, I ween!
Deep purple shadows falling here and there,
　Quiet winding rivers, slopes of living green,
Long sweeps of silver sand that stretched away
Round the wide circle of the sleeping bay.

III.

The long white rollers, beating on the reef,
　Made deep, wild music; and the landward breeze
(Breathing so low as scarce to stir a leaf),
　Bore the long boom back o'er the sleeping seas;

And the sweet twilight (all, alas! too brief)

    Cast long, soft shadows through the whispering trees,

That towered aloft, great pillars clothed with green,

With winding aisles of sweetest glades between.

IV.

And flowers of gorgeous hue, and wondrous form,

    Opened to night's soft touch on fairy bowers,

Living their short rich life; for ere the morn

    Those fragile gems had lived their few sweet hours;

But e'en decay did bring no cause to mourn,

    For with the dawn, and dawn's bright sparkling showers,

There burst to life new flowers on every spray,

That charmed each sense through all the live-long day.

V.

And from each peak (high clothed in deepest green,
　E'en to the summit) there did always flash,
Swift leaping streams of purest silver sheen,
　That made short pause, then down the gorge would dash—
So deep and sheer—the falling shower was seen
　To melt in rainbow mist—nor ever lash
The great dark rocks below, but only fell
In golden mist, far, far adown the dell.

VI.

Then through the fertile plain the river wound,
　Slowly and silent seaward, and I ween
Sweet on the listening ear did fall the sound
　Of chanted song—the singers all unseen—

Hid by the drooping trees, as, seaward bound,

    The light canoe, through walls of living green,

Bore its light-hearted crew to jest and play

On the long rolling surges of the bay.

VII.

There would they pause, each happy, laughing face,

    Waiting the highest wave that landward swept;

Then with a merry shout began the race,

    As the huge rolling billow onward leapt;

Each swimmer flying with the lightning's pace,

    Poised on the buoyant wave, and deftly kept

Fair on the sparkling crest, and light and free,

As sea-gulls sweeping o'er a summer sea.

VIII.

On! while the gazer views with trembling eye,

    The lessening distance, where with thunderous shock

The crashing billows dash and leap on high,

    Against the frowning cliff and cruel rock,

Where they who strike must on the instant die;

    And where the mighty surge would only mock

Man's puny strength, and cast him forth to bleed,

Lifeless and shattered like a worthless weed.

IX.

But see! within one instant of such death!

    As makes the boldest shudder but to see!

A sudden plunge—a sudden, quick-drawn breath,

    And every swimmer sinks beneath the sea;

And then like Tritons flashing far beneath,

    Seaward through silent, sparkling depths they flee,

Fearless as ocean's silvery brood, that flies

Before those flashing arms and sparkling eyes.

X.

So speeds with varied sport the tropic day,

    The shadows gather, and the balmy night

Calls back the wanderers to the dance and play,

    Where sparkles many a home-fire warm and bright

Where loving hands the light repast would lay,

    And hail the truant back with love's delight;

And friend meet friend with kindly word and smile,

And rest and sleep brood softly o'er the isle.

XI.

And who shall dare to say the white man's hand
  Changed for the better all this simple life?
He came and found a fair and happy land,
  Abundance left no cause for crime and strife.
What is it now? Go ask the lonely sand!
  What is it now? Go see where crime is rife!
Few! few! are left, and these are but a shame,
A slander on the race from which they came!

XII.

Where is the stalwart form and fearless eye?
  Where is the simple virtue of the child?
Where is the courage that could dare and die
  For love or friendship? Ask the silent wild!

For there in lowly graves the sleepers lie,
   Who faded fast, o'erborne, unreconciled
With the new life, new modes, new thoughts, new creeds,
Which held their virtues even—worthless weeds!

XIII.

And what remains? A better, purer life?
   Their outraged ancestors would thunder " No!"
Cunning, deceit, unfaith, these! these are rife,
   With all their springs of being running low;
Unfit for action, unprepared for strife,
   Lost to their ancient manhood; with a show
Of seeming knowledge, which they cannot use,
Of seeming virtue, which they but abuse.

XIV.

Where was the fault ?   Is Christian teaching wrong?

　Is all our boasted knowledge but a name?

Knowledge that we have learned through ages long,

　From the world's history, blazoned o'er with fame

Of noble deeds, of art, of gifted song,

　Of purest virtue, and with many a name

Of saint and martyr, suffering death that we

Might hold our birthright, freest of the free ?

XV.

Nay ! what is true is true—but many an age

　Has slowly built our knowledge ; stone by stone

The mighty structure rose; and page by page
    We learned our lesson through the ages gone;
Our race has risen toiling stage by stage;
    It took a century for one step alone;
God worketh not in haste, and we must know
What is of God, to finite man seems slow!

XVI.

And thus we erred, we undertook to teach
    And change a race, by hotbed culture, when
We should have been content to slowly reach
    The goal by law of God, and not of men!
Hastening no violent change by deed or speech,
    Teaching reforms within their simple ken,
Saving such things as suited race and clime,
Leaving the harvest unto God's own time.

XVII.

Not so we acted! In a few short years,
  Spurious reform had taken all they had
Of the old régime. On their hopes and fears
  We should have built, not driven them mad
With a mock liberty. Ah me, the tears!
  The dreary land, the wailing long and sad!
That we have caused. Wait, bigot, 'twill be told
When the dread record is at last unrolled!

XVIII.

A simple nation, ruled by simple laws,
  And stern old customs, that to them were life!
Grant it was despotism, grant the flaws,
  Which we the enlightened saw were all too rife;

Yet that same despotism was the cause

   Of their prosperity; and crime and strife

Met with their swift reward ; and so was taught

That virtue, without which all else is naught :

XIX.

Obedience !—the obedience of the child.

   And it was well, for those who ruled were wise ;

Wise in their day, and ruled their vassals wild,

   With a wild wisdom.   Had we learned to prize

Those simple feudal laws, both stern and mild,

   And been not over hasty to despise,

Perchance we had not dug a nation's grave,

Nor slain the kindly race we came to save.

XX.

'Tis past ! The record now is all with God !

The past can never be recalled again ;

The sea they sported on, the land they trod,

Shall see them never more ! their joy and pain

Are all laid low beneath their native sod !

Another race their lovely land has ta'en ;

And the far peaks, sweet streams, and gleaming shore,

Shall echo back their songs no more—no more !

CAPTAIN TEACH.

ANNO DOMINI, 1719.

WHERE the great magnolia trees,

Kiss the sleeping summer seas,

And their perfume floats out softly, o'er the shimmering

Bocca Grand;

Where the drooping fronds of palm,

Whisper through the tropic calm,

Lay Teach, the pirate Captain, with his anchor on the

sand.

On the larboard lay the land,

On the starboard shoals of sand,

While away beyond the breakers leapt with sullen moan

and cry:

And the sweep of land and bay,

Stretched for leagues and leagues away,

Till the low, long, winding headland touched the arches

of the sky.

On the Bocca calm and blue,

Lay the pirate and his crew,

With his evil-gotten treasure, and his evil-gotten fame;

Little dreaming of the fate,

Coming sure, though coming late,

By the hands of England's Captain, of unsullied soul and

name.

Sir Robert Mayne came sailing—

With brave hearts that knew no failing,

Hearts reared in merry England, the birthland of the free—

In the good ship *England's Glory*—

Famed in many a song and story—

With her pennant, like a sea-bird's wing, out-streaming on the lee.

"Shot the guns, run out the guards;

Strike the topmasts, trim the yards—

I am ready for the devil! and for all his English crew!—

Aim your longest cannon there!

Sight it true, and sight it fair—

A chest of Spanish silver for the first shot through and through!"

Thus spoke the pirate Teach,

In his boastful, vaunting speech,

Like an evil-minded braggart, with an evil heart and soul.

But his hour of doom was nigh,

And the day that he must die

Had dawned on land and ocean—his day of doom and dole.

Spoke Sir Robert, calm and slow,

"Men of mine, who fear no foe,

Many a fight we've fought together, many a long and hard-won fight!

Men of mine, for love of wives—

For the sake of seamen's lives—

We must stop this braggart's vaunting, ere the day goes down in night!"

And they answered with a cheer,

Answered without doubt or fear,

Answered gallantly and gaily, in their quaintly sailor speech :

"Aye, aye, Sir Robert, aye !

We are ready all this day,

To ornament our yard-arm with this caitiff pirate Teach !"

And the ships like living things,

With quivering, half-shut wings,

Drew slowly, slowly nearer, in their grand and stately pride,

Till they almost locked their yards,

Almost touched their nets and guards,

Till they lay in sullen silence, darkly towering side by side.

Hailed Sir Robert from the rail,

With a clear and courtly hail,

"Captain Teach, I come to fight you in a fair and open fight!

I will neither ask nor give

Truce nor quarter while I live;

You or I must end our sailing, and God prosper who is right!"

Then the deadly fight began,

Gun to gun, and man to man;

And a smoke like hell o'ergathered, lightened only by the glare

Of the cannon's deadly breath,

Flashing through the gloom of death;

And no arm but struck its hardest, and no lip asked quarter there!

The sun grew red o'erhead,

Glaring ghastly on the dead,

Through the rolling smoke of battle—and the sea breeze

died away;

While the ships, all maimed and scarred,

Lay with shattered mast and yard,

But the deadly battle stayed not through the long hot

tropic day.

And the sea was stained with red,

By the wounded and the dead,

And one half Sir Robert's sailors would fight or sail no

more!

Still the fight—nor lost nor won

At the setting of the sun—

Thundered o'er the shimmering Bocca from its furthest

shore to shore.

And all through the tropic night

Crashed the horror of the fight,

But near dawn of day the cannon slackened—ceased—

and spake no more !

And through the yawning hatch—

In his hand a lighted match—

Leapt Teach, the pirate captain, stark and ghastly,

wounded sore !

One moment through the ship

(With a curse upon his lip)

He gazed on wrack and ruin, men torn by shot and fire ;

On comrades true and tried,

Crushed and mangled side by side !

Then turned him to his purpose, with a spirit fierce and

dire.

And he split the ship in twain,

From the keelson to the main,

And a lurid light rushed upward like a baleful shooting star;

And the ship sank down like lead,

With its dying and its dead,

While the ocean surged and trembled, and the echoes rolled afar!

So the direful deed was done,

And the fight nor lost nor won!

And Sir Robert with his living few, and with his many dead;

Cleared away the shattered wreck,

From his grim and ghastly deck,

While the shot-torn flag of England still floated overhead.

Then with reverence and with care,

With a sailor's shrift and prayer,

In a sailor's shroud wound meetly, beneath the tropic deep

Sir Robert laid his dead,

With a shot at feet and head—

Laid his gallant English sailors to their last long quiet sleep.

And he slowly sailed away

From the sad and silent bay,

With his shot-rent ship and wounded men, the fearless and the true.

And the good ship *England's Glory*,

Still lives in song and story,

For the victory won, and good deed done, and gallant English crew.

Still the Bocca Grand is bright,

Shimmering through the tropic night;

Still the palm-trees droop and whisper, still the great magnolias sweep;

Still the breakers moan and cry,

Still the low winds creep and sigh;

Still the headlands guard and shelter, where the long-dead sailors sleep.

THE WHALER "DEVONPORT."

A YARN OF THE DOG-WATCH, FOUNDED ON FACT.

Shipmates, 'twas thirty years agone, mayhap 'twas somewhat more,

I sailed in the whaler *Devonport*, from England's bonnie shore,

In the month o' May, when hawthorns bloom, an' merry cuckoos call,

When throstles build, an' cowslips blow, an' apple-blossoms fall.

My father farmed in Devon, an' I was his only lad,

But I caught the glamour o' the sea, an' my heart grew hot an' mad,

With the tales the seamen told me o' a broader earth an'
    sky,
Where youth's dreams had freer action, where the blessèd
    islands lie.

I left my weeping mother an' my sisters—silly fool!
Ah! it's many a long year, shipmates, since my head had
    time to cool;
But the glamour o' the ocean holds me yet; I cannot
    sleep
If I do not feel the motion, hear the moaning o' the
    deep.

Oh! the bonnie white-caps leaping with a merry all-sail
    breeze,
O! the mystery an' the beauty o' the night in tropic seas;

O ! the ecstasy o' flying when the storm-wrack wails an' cries,
An' day an' night are all as one, in leaden-coloured skies.

Some live upon the land an' die, an' then are laid to rest,
Beside the dear old village church in ground that has been blest;
But, shipmates, when my watch is called, no dreary ground for me,
But a grave a thousand fathoms deep, beneath the tropic sea !

A bed upon the coral sand, where colours warm an' bright,
Will shimmer round me all the day, an' stars through all the night ;

Where I'll hear the ocean voices,—faint an' far the breaker's roar,
Floating softly on the night-wind, from some palm-encircled shore.

'Twas hereabout—some twenty south—the trades had died away,
The ship was heading east-by-south, with hardly steering way;
We were keeping lively sharp look-outs, for one more whale or so
Would send the old craft bowling home, a full ship high an' low.

We were clear of all the islands, an' the long Pacific swell—
Like the rolling downs of Devon—from the southward rose an' fell;

Eight bells had gone, the starboard watch had hardly gone below,
When the merry hail from mast-head came, "There! there again they blow!"

There was rattling o' the boat-falls by stout willing hands that day,
While the captain hailed the mast-heads, "Where away, lads, where away?"
"On the larboard bow, two points or so, where the clouds are lowering rain,
Pull north-by-east will head them, sir; an' there! an' there again!"

'Twas a long stiff pull to windward, but the signal came at last,
As the tropic sun had almost set, "The captain's boat is fast;

The third mate fouled and cut his line, but the captain's whale is dead;
An' now they've got their tow-lines out; 'bout ship, sir, slue her head!"

Our mate was dark an' sullen—French or Spanish—with an eye
Where foul shadows, lust an' murder, an' all evil passions lie;
We lost our good old English mate—true heart and brave, he lies
Where the sullen icebergs plunge an' roll, an' the north wind moans an' cries.

"'Bout ship! 'bout ship! the boats are here, away abaft the beam;
I see them as they rise an' fall, where the setting sun-rays gleam.

'Bout ship, sir! board the starboard tacks, she'll fetch up
nor'-nor'-west;
Brace sharp an' close an' shave the wind, due north would fetch 'em best."

"Steady, you lubber! steady there! an' keep her full-an'-by!"
Our mate, the villain, thundered, with foul murder in his eye.
Shipmates, 'tis thirty years agone! but now as plain as then,
I see that night, our ship, the mate, an' horror-stricken men!

No other word was spoken—I stood my weary wheel,
But Lord forefend I evermore such dreary watch may feel!

All through the long soft tropic night, each sailor kept his place,
With soul filled full o' fear an' hate, an' horror-stricken face.

You see the boys an' oldish men were left to keep the ship,
An' the mate we feared an' hated, an' no question passed a lip;
But we knew, full well we knew it all—'twas passed from eye to eye—
Our shipmates an' our brave old man, were foully left to die!

The breeze grew stiff at sunrise, an' by noon we had a gale,
An' were flying like a frightened gull, ere the mate would shorten sail;

And then we lost our royals, when at last we tried to clew;
And the mainsail left the bolt-ropes, an' the foresail split in two.

He never dared to heave her to; by day an' night we fled,
The mountain waves behind us, an' the flying foam ahead;
The villain feared to tarry, for the fiend was near him then,
An' behind (close following in our wake), the ghosts of murdered men!

An' so an evil-haunted ship, for seven dark days we flew,
Two men lashed always at the wheel, for fear o' broaching to;

For seven long dreary days we fled, no stitch on either mast,

An' yet they bent an' swayed an' swung, like reeds before the blast.

An' then we made the Spanish coast, by Talcahuano Bay,

An' the Spanish pilot boarded, but no word we dared to say,

For you know that logs are made to lie, and how the Lord were we

To prove our mates were left to die, on that far lonely sea?

We took our chance an' bolted—bolted every man an' lad !

Wandered north to Valparaiso, an' a dreary time we had.

The Dons are very civil, if your pocket's lined with gold;
But they always were a cruel set, an' charity is cold!

Some shipped an' sailed for England, an' we scattered far an' wide,
Scattered like the sea-foam flying, as fate chances to betide
A sailor's fitful voyage, wandering always near an' far,
From the lanes that bound his village, to the furthest setting star.

Shipmates, out here, when storms are wild, two boats are sometimes seen,
With sails an' oars an' signal-waif, an' tow-line stretched between;

Mann'd by a crew of skeletons, with fleshless fingers pressed

On the weary oar, till they sail no more, an' God shall give them rest.

I saw them once! an' th' moonlight gleamed in their white bones through and through,

May the good Lord grant I nevermore behold that ghastly crew!

'Tis a weird an' awful omen; an' should they chance to hail,

Your ship, however stout an' strong, will founder in the gale.

"Relieve the wheel, and set the watch!" "Aye, aye, sir." Lord, how strange!

The present drives the past away, with all its time and change.

All past and gone! all past and gone! an' thirty years an' more
Since I sailed in the whaler *Devonport* from England's bonnie shore!

WITH FRANKY DRAKE.

IN THE YEAR OF GRACE FIFTEEN HUNDRED AND EIGHTY-FOUR.

I SAILED with Franky Drake, in fifteen eighty-four,
I sailed with Franky Drake, fair and free;
    We muster'd just four-score,
    When we stood out from the Nore,
    Stauncher men ne'er sailed before
        Over sea.

We cruised off Margarita, and took a town or two,
And lined our pockets well with Spanish gold;
  Then our captain, bold and true,
  Said, "My lads, this will not do;
  We grow fat, my valiant crew,
    Fat and old.

"My merry masters all, we grow fat and we grow tame,
In this life of little battles and of sloth!
  We must find us work and fame,
  Worthy of our ancient name;
  With this lazy life of shame
    I am wroth!

"In Santa Martha Bay, four galleons that I ken,
Are loaded deep with bars of Spanish gold;
 Each rates two hundred men—
 Eight hundred!—Well, what then?
 We are safe with one to ten,
  Comrades bold!"

And we answered, "Ready all, gallant Franky! as you please
We will follow, captain ours, where'er we may!"
 And we up before the breeze,
 As it kissed the spicy trees,
 And across the Indian seas
  Slid away.

We rounded Cape Gallinas as the tropic sun sank
low,

And by dawn we had the pretty birds in sight,

 All sailing in a row,

 With their wings like drifted snow,

 And their carronades aglow

  In the light.

With their long, low Spanish lines, and their banners
trailing free,

And their double tier of guns run fiercely out ;

 While they hailed us o'er the sea,

 Grandly asking who were we !

 And we answered on the lee

  With a shout,

"We be men of merry Devon! we be all true Englishmen,"

And their cannon thundered fiercely in reply;

    So we fought them there and then,

    Fought them gaily one to ten!

    Fought them, knowing like true men

        How to die.

So we laughed and fought away, and many wounded sore,

Never murmured in their last and awful need;

    But when the fight was o'er,

    We mustered not four-score!

    But men ne'er did before

        A braver deed.

And the Dons struck flags at last from every tapering mast,

Struck flags and yielded in their stately way;

 And many a brave soul passed,

 Many a stout lad fought his last,

 While the cannon thundered fast

  On that day.

And 'twas wondrous fair, I ween, all the gorgeous jewels there,

And the golden bars that glittered in the hold!

 Great heaps so pure and fair,

 You could see your shadow there,

 A wondrous sight and rare,

  Of wealth untold!

WITH FRANKY DRAKE.

So we took great spoil of jewels, and we took great spoil

of gold,

But great glory was the spoil we most did take,

In the merry days of old,

When we did as we were told,

When we sailed so free and bold

With Franky Drake.

ISANDLANA.

(Fought January 22nd, 1879.)

FOR QUEEN AND COUNTRY.

I.

Hail to the dead who fell on that dread morning,
    Their foes a score to one;
Shoulder to shoulder, flight or rescue scorning,
    Brave hearts and true, well done!

II.

Hemmed by that wall of foes, fierce, mad, appalling,
    With murder writtten there,
Stood friend by friend, and soothed each comrade falling,
    With soldier's shrift and prayer.

III.

Rose the dead higher, round their lessening number,

    Still narrower grew the space;

Each cheering each—work first, then blessèd slumber—

    While calmer grew each face.

IV.

Calmer and purer, and a wondrous beauty

    Filled each flashing eye;

For " Queen and country " and that watchword " duty,"

    Ready for these to die!

V.

Flashed thoughts away to old remembered places,

    To those who wait in vain;

To the last words, the smiles, the tear-dimmed faces

    They ne'er shall see again!

VI.

To English hedgerows, Scottish hills of heather,
    Old Erin's emerald sod;
The Sabbath bells, the worshippers together
    Chanting their hymns to God.

VII.

All the old memories for one moment blending,
    One moment wild and deep;
Like years of common pain, the heart-strings rending,
    And then?—hush! then to sleep.

VIII.

Oh, English hearts! where'er you be, remember
    'Tis well to weep and pray,
For the brave men, the brave, the true, the tender,
    Who died on that dread day.

IN MEMORIAM.

PRINCE IMPERIAL; KILLED JUNE 1ST, 1879.

I.

Droop England's flag half-mast; sail soft and slowly,
  Oh! ship, with thy sad freight.
Bear him with reverent hands—who lieth lowly—
  Back to his mother's gate.

II.

Speak not of comfort to the stricken mother;
  Silence and tears are best;
Bear him, as soldiers bear an honoured brother,
  Then leave him to his rest.

III.

Toll thy bells, England! 'tis a fitting requiem,
   For him so young and brave;
Let silent crowds in reverence receive him
    Back to an English grave.

IV.

Peal the sad cannon forth in solemn thunder,
   Chant the low prayer to God;
Lay the pale brow, the blood-stained bosom, under
    Our peaceful English sod.

V.

Remember that he died for England's glory,
   In England's quarrel fell;
And when in sunny France you tell the story,
    Say, England loved him well!

VI.

Loved him and did him honour, as was seemly,
  Who broke so brave a lance;
And England's Queen, both womanly and queenly,
  Wept for the heir of France.

VII.

He may not sleep in his fair land of roses,
  Where hangs the laden vine;
But we shall guard him well, where he reposes,
  Beneath our Northern pine.

FOUNDERED IN THE JAVA SEA

ANNO DOMINI 1879.

A SEA of glass—a silent cape,

Close fringed with palms from shore to shore;

A rose-hued cloud of awful shape;

    A whisper and no more

Of unformed sound, that stirs the air,

So faint and far, you know not where.

White useless sails against the masts,

That move not, hanging idly there;

A sun that ne'er a shadow casts,

    Only a sullen glare;

No life, no motion, and no sound;

To the horizon's utmost bound!

A breathless waiting for the spell,

Of the weird restless rest to break;

Lips white with what they cannot tell,

    Stout hearts that almost quake

With a strange unaccustomed fear,

To stand so still, with death so near.

A sea-bird rushing to the land

(Where the long palm-fronds droop and swing),

So fearless, that the outstretched hand

    Could touch the quivering wing;

The poor wild heart, and gleaming eye,

Fearless of man who too must die.

A long low band that stretches o'er

The sullen sea—as still as death,

A silent sea—a silent shore!

    And then the stifled breath;

The first hot breath—so faint—it fails

To stir the half-spread drooping sails.

A lurid flash! and sea and sky

Meet in one hue of dusky gloom,

A crash of spars—a human cry!

    Amid the wrack of doom—

Then but the wailing of the wind

O'er eyes that are for ever blind!

THE SPANISH CAPTAIN.

I.

OH ! for the days of chivalry, oh ! for the gallant men !

Who fought and always conquered, though the odds were one to ten !

For the days when Spain was mistress where'er her flag unfurled,

And our good swords, five hundred strong, subdued the southern world !

II.

We sailed with good Balboa, we crossed the Indian sea,

We landed at the isthmus; oh, a gallant band were we !

All men of spotless lineage from our brave captain down,
All cavaliers of honour, all names of old renown!

III.

We burned our ships behind us, for we never meant to flee,
We turned our faces westward,—westward to the unknown sea;
Onward through silent forests, through deadly swamps all day,
But the highness of our courage kept the fever-fiend at bay!

IV.

Battles with countless hosts by day, by night the quick surprise,

When the stealthy foe were only seen by the glitter of their eyes!

And the silent, deadly arrows, that fell like tropic showers,

From swamp and thicket, cliff and tree, through all night's creeping hours.

V.

But at last, at last, the ocean burst upon our raptured sight,

The mighty "Mar del sur" in all its mystery and its might;

Far stretching to the westward, only bounded by the sun,

And this our swords had conquered! this our toiling hands had won!

VI.

Strode our chief in all his armour, with a proudly flashing eye,

Boldly waist-deep in the ocean, with Spain's banner waving high!

With his silent knights around him, few, but in their might a host;

And out spake our gallant captain, while the breeze Spain's banner tost.

VII.

"In the name of God the highest! by the grace of His dear Son,

(Who has brought us here, my comrades, who has all our battles won);

In the name of our dear Lady (by whose prayers we have been kept

When our wounded hands were fighting, when our weary eyes have slept).

VIII.

"I do take this southern ocean, I do take this southern land!

With its islands, with its rivers, with its wondrous golden sand!

For our king and his for ever! May his hand have strength from heaven
To keep against all comers what our blessèd Lord has given!"

IX.

On our knees beneath the palm-trees, humbly knelt each soldier then,
While arose in solemn measure from each lip the deep "Amen;"
And the blood-red sun sank slowly down beyond the southern main,
And flashed with streams of glory on the brave old flag of Spain!

X.

Oh, for the days of chivalry! oh, for the gallant men!

Who fought and always conquered, though the odds were one to ten!

For the days when Spain was mistress where'er her flag unfurled,

And our good swords, five hundred strong, subdued the southern world!

CLOTHO.

I.

A BRAVE knight rode to the wars away,
  (Oh, never a cloud in the east or west!)
His hopes were high, and his heart was gay,
  (The sun glints fair on a soldier's crest.)

II.

A lady is weeping and wringing her hands,
  (The clouds grow dark as the year grows old.)
And the lady is thinking of blood-stained lands;
  (And a knight lies silent and stark and cold.)

III.

A ship sailed out, most wondrous fair,

    (Oh, merry the sea-gulls wheel and rise!)

But the sea cares not for moan or prayer;

    (Oh, wild white moon in the pitiless skies!)

IV.

A woman is wailing and rending her hair,

    (The sea-weed twines where the sleeper lies.)

Be still! for the sea hears not despair;

    (False wind that whispers, false wind that cries!)

V.

Two lovers with hands and lips close pressed;

    (The nightingales pipe in the hawthorn sweet.)

Make room, oh dead, for another guest!

    (Lay rue and myrrh at the small white feet.)

VI.

A mother is kissing her babe's sweet face,

    (Daffodils, violets, blue and white.)

The felon had once such a tender grace—

    (Back to the shadow, oh bird of the night!)

VII.

Brave young hearts, and strong young hands,

    (Poppies aglow in the morning sun.)

Unmarked graves in far-off lands,

    (Oh sweet, sweet sleep when the work is done!)

VIII.

Strong swift feet at the dawning of light,

    (The dew hangs bright on the eglantine.)

Slow feet creeping to rest at night,

    (The wind moans deep in the spores o' the pine.)

CHANGE.

I.

Oh! wild birds sing to me a strain,
    The old familiar blessèd lays;
Oh! fill my heart with joy and pain,
    And so bring back the vanished days.

II.

While here I lie upon the grass,
    And the old trees their shadows fling;
And clouds across the blue sky pass,
    Oh! wild birds sing, oh! wild birds sing.

III.

Bring back, bring back, the vanished years,

    Oh! bring me back one vanished face

I lost in that thick mist of tears;

    Fill once again her vacant place.

IV.

Once more, once more, oh! bring once more,

    To my cold heart the swell and glow,

That dear voice brought in days of yore;

    Sing low, sweet birds, sing soft and low!

V.

Bring back, bring back, the olden time,

    When we were children, she and I,

And life was one long rush of rhyme;

    Ah! sing dear birds, sing clear and high!

VI.

Time creeps or flies, and all things change;
    Who keepeth aught of all he had?
The dear old dreams grow cold and strange;
    Sing low, sweet birds, sing low and sad!

VII.

And who hath done what once he planned,
    When first he gaily hoisted sail,
And shaped his course for his dreamland?
    Ah! wild birds droop your wings and wail!

VIII.

All—all that course is scattered o'er
    With cold, dead hopes that shrouded lie,
Whose wailing ghosts for evermore
    Haunt our slow steps, and moan and cry!

IX.

With outstretched hands, in dark and gloom,
   We grope our way, we know not where;
Uncertain shades beside a tomb;
   Oh! birds your wailing seems despair!

X.

The shadows fall and day is past,
   The cold white moon gleams o'er the hill;
The last faint whispering notes—the last!
   Tremble and cease, and all is still.

MY SHIP.

My ship sailed out (oh heart, be still!), sailed out o'er Humber bar,
Sailed bravely out in the dawning light, beneath the morning star.
A stronger ship ne'er crossed the sea, nor crew with stouter will;
But ten long years is a weary time! (be still, oh heart, be still!)

My years were few, my love was true, I laughed at time and fears;
What though the days grew into months, and the months grew into years!

MY SHIP.

(Lie still, poor heart, and let me speak!) I knew—full
 well I knew
That let betide what might betide, my sailor's heart was
 true!

I dreamed by night of far-off lands, strange lands of palm
 and gold,
But it never entered my silly head that years make all
 grow old!
(Be still, oh heart!) And I woke each dawn, with a song
 upon my lip,
And watched all day in storm and calm, for the coming
 of my ship.

And so the cruel years went past, uncounted all by
 me,
What would I care for a score of years when my lad
 came back from sea!

What would I care! (oh, foolish heart, why will you flutter so?
When you woke and knew it was all a dream, full twenty years ago!).

At last one morning (oh, sweet blue sky, that never shone again!)
My ship came over Humber bar, and I heard the anchor chain;
My lips were waiting for his dear lips, but he passed me by instead!
And a great gulf swallowed the earth and sky, and I thought that God was dead!

You see I was but a silly lass, and love my only thought;
I never knew that hearts could change, or love be sold or bought!

But men love not as women love! (poor heart, it could not be),

And oh, would God that I had died when my lad went off to sea!

THE ROLL-CALL.

I.

Now the fierce charge is past,

Shrill rings the trumpet blast,

Now count the cost at last,

    Comrade and brother!

Down in the bloody snow,

Those who an hour ago

Charged through the broken foe,

    Cheering each other!

II.

Ah! the good sight and brave,
As plume and sabre wave,
Charging to find a grave,
    Through smoke of battle:
Hearts beating wild and high,
Ready to do or die,
Soldier's short prayer and sigh,
    Then bayonets' rattle!

III.

Down! down the foremost rank,
Line after line a blank,
Down plume and helm sank,
    Down, down to slumber.

Trampled by horse and man,

Ah! the brave blood that ran!

Oh! tell the woe who can!

    Now count the number!

IV.

Yes!—count each empty place,

Yes!—count each missing face,

Who foremost in that race,

    Fell crowned with glory;

Who struck the foremost blow,

Who deepest charged the foe,

Who lieth stark and low,

    Lies crushed and gory!

V.

Ah, yes! but who can say,

Who count what hearts this day—

Hearts that were light and gay—

    Now shall be broken?

Who tell what faces fair,

Shall fade with wild despair,

Who hear the wailing prayer

    That shall be spoken?

VI.

Now the fierce charge is past,

Shrill rings the trumpet blast,

Now count the cost at last,

    Comrade and brother!

THE ROLL-CALL.

Down in the bloody snow,

Those who, an hour ago,

Charged through the broken foe,

  Cheering each other!

DRIFTING APART.

I.

DRIFTING apart in the cruel years,

    Drifting apart on the sea of time ;

Eyes that are dim with their frozen tears,

    Hearts far away, though the hands reach mine ;

Sorrow of sorrows too great for speech !—

    That through all the years that are yet to come—

Our souls are hidden away from each,

    And our hearts may break, but our lips are dumb !

II.

Drifting apart, in no storm of hate,
    Drifting apart 'neath a tranquil sky;
The moan in our hearts, too late! too late!
    Our poor lips white with the stifled cry;
Our hands outspread, but we only reach
    Hands! not the hearts we would die to keep!
Oh! sorrow of sorrows too great for speech,
    Oh! sorrow as deep as the grave is deep!

III.

Drifting apart, on a fathomless sea,
    A sea where no anchor can hold or save;
Where the face of our dead we are doomed to see,
    For ever unhid by the merciful grave;

And their unclosed eyes, so near! so near!
   That we read their story of long despair;
Poor eyes that have lost all hope and fear
   Of the years to come, or the years that were.

IV.

Drifting apart, to meet no more,
   No more!—till the sea gives up its dead;
Till our feet shall touch that far sweet shore,
   Where the lotos for rue shall bloom instead;
Where the old sweet time of the long, long past!
   Shall grow in our hearts, and the cruel sea
Shall hear and obey, at last! at last!
   And the drifting and moaning shall no more be.

THE LOTUS.

Ah, wondrous flower! fair mystic flower
    Oh, cast your magic o'er my heart!
The weary toil, the lust of power,
    Oh, lotus, bid them all depart!
And give me of your priceless balm,
    The perfect bliss of perfect calm!

Oh! sweetest flower that ever grew
    Beneath the circle of the sun;
With spells the magi never knew—
    Knowledge and power they never won—
Heal with your touch my drooping hands,
    And teach me where Nirvana stands.

Ah, bid my weary heart no more
    Wander o'er earth from birth to death!
And vainly seek from shore to shore,
    The boon I crave of thy sweet breath—
Surcease from joy! surcease from pain!
    And ne'er to moan or laugh again!

Teach me the secret I have sought
    On every land, on every sea;
The lesson wisdom never taught
    Since mortal touched the fatal tree;
The secret lost, when through the gate—
    Weeping—passed Adam desolate!

Oh, spirit of the priceless gift!
    Heal with your light my blinded eyes,
The awful veil of sorrow lift,
    And show beyond—your tranquil skies,

Where death, and life, shall but appear

    A far-off dream from year to year.

A far-off dream! so very far

    That all death's darkness, life's despair,

All unsolved mysteries that are,

    Shall only blend to music there;

And thou shalt reign a queen in power,

    Spirit of rest! sweet lotus flower!

ELUIA.

I never knew you loved me,
        Eluia!
I never knew you loved me,
        Never knew!
Though I saw the flashing gleams
Light your eyes with tender beams,
I thought 'twas only dreams
        Flashing through.

Your eyes were like the night,

    Eluia!

Your eyes were like the night,

      Sweet and true!

Where I watched the lightning dart,

But our thoughts were far apart,

And your breaking love-slain heart

      I never knew!

I thought you were a child,

    Eluia!

I thought you were a child,

      All fancy free;

But a woman's heart was there,

Breaking with a wild despair,

Yet the sweet love true and fair

      I could not see.

Thou art sleeping quietly now,

   Eluia!

Thou art sleeping quietly now,

    At peace for aye!

And with footsteps sad and slow—

With a heart o'erwhelmed with woe—

On a darkened path I go

    My weary way.

The palm-trees whisper still,

   Eluia!

The palm-trees whisper still

    Beside the sea;

And the waves still kiss the shore,

Laughing as in days of yore,

But the past can come no more

    To you and me!

GHOSTS.

A SONG OF THE OLD YEAR.

Only the flickering fire-light in my room,
  Only bells tolling for the dying year;
Only the silence and the midnight gloom,
    And then my ghosts appear!

They ope no door, no quick or heavy tread
  Crosses my threshold with a rude foot-fall;
But with the grace and reverence of the dead,
    They enter softly all.

Enter and take their places by my chair;

    Enter and touch me with their shadowy hands;

Bringing the light and darkness, joy and care,

        From other years and lands.

And once again I dream youth's wayward dream,

    And look once more in long, long closèd eyes;

And once again the hues of Eden gleam

        In vanished sunset skies.

And words are spoken in my lonely room,

    Sweet words—so low—my heart alone can hear—

By lips that have been silent in the tomb,

        Silent for many a year!

And once again a summer day has birth,

    Of such a glory over land and sea,

  As ne'er again shall dawn upon this earth!

        Shall dawn no more for me.

And on my hands soft loving hands are laid,

    And o'er my face the tears of parting fall,

  And through my room's uncertain light and shade,

        Old voices moan and call!

Only the flickering fire-light in my room,

    Only bells tolling for the dying year;

  Only the silence and the midnight gloom,

        And then my ghosts appear!

THE OLD LOVE.

I.

Oh! for the love—the old, old love! and the love that shone like a star,

That loved for the sweet dear sake of love, in the land I have left afar;

Oh! for the whispers well understood, though never a word was told,

And oh! for the touch of a true, true hand, that was mine in the days of old.

II.

Past—past—past! all past and dead, and buried for ever and aye,

No token left of the golden dream, that seemed so real that day;

Oh! had I known life's wayward stream, and watched as the years rushed past,

Perchance I had seen where the dark rocks lay, and saved my love at last.

III.

But life is cruel, and time is swift, and the past beyond recall,

And we learn too late that love—sweet love! is the one great prize of all;

And youth is vain in its strength and pride, and we heed not the pilot star,

Till a voice moans back, "Too late—too late!" from the land we have left afar.

IV.

The tears are past, and the pain is past, and the sudden midnight cry,

The shadows are lengthening long and fast, the sun hangs low in the sky;

I count the journey by steps—not leagues! I hear the infinite sea;

But the dream I dreamt in the years that are dead, is the same sweet dream to me.

V.

Oh! for the love—the old, old love! and the love that shone like a star,

That loved for the sweet dear sake of love, in the land I have left afar;

Oh! for the whispers well understood, though never a word was told,

And oh! for the touch of a true, true hand, that was mine in the days of old.

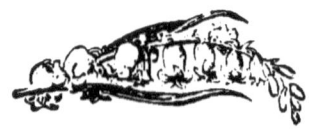

DEAD.

I.

Dead! he is dead we say, and veil our faces,
    And our poor hearts stand still;
Dreading to turn and see the vacant places,
    This earth can no more fill.

II.

Dead! he is dead in spite of all our keeping—
    In spite of close-shut door—
Gone! he is gone beyond our wail and weeping;
    Never to enter more

III.

Within our chambers, or to hear our greetings,
    With the old tender ways;
No more sad partings, ah! no more glad meetings,
    Through all life's weary days!

IV.

And now our hearts "go softly," bowed and broken,
    Through all the future years;
Spring blooms and fades, but brings to us no token,
    No touch to heal our tears.

V.

Ah! if our darkened hearts could but discover
    That he we say is dead,
Had passed (as babe on breast of sweetest mother)
    To perfect life instead!

VI.

To life that will be new, when the far ages
>Shall hear the crack of doom;
To life! with which the brightest dreams of sages
>Were only dreams of gloom;

VII.

To rest—to rest—ah me! such rest as never
>Was found on sea or land;
Where no tears fall, where speechless lips ne'er quiver,
>Kissing some poor cold hand!

VIII.

Yea! could we see beyond the tears and crying,
>See the sweet rest instead;
Oh! if we knew 'twas living, and not dying!
>We dare not whisper—"Dead!"

WAITING.

I.

A SHIP unmoored in the dawning light,
    Her white sails shimmered, her flag flowed free;
And hearts were merry, and eyes were bright,
    For the wraith that is near us we cannot see!
Oh, the weary nights, and the lagging years!
    Waiting, and watching the treacherous wave;
The heart that is broken can shed no tears,
    And why must we toil so long for a grave?

II.

All things were merry that summer morn,
 The bells, and the birds, and the laughing sea;
The sweet wind rustled through waving corn:
 Oh, wind that has stolen my love from me!
Oh, the weary nights, and the lagging years!
 Waiting, and watching the treacherous wave;
The heart that is broken can shed no tears,
 And why must we toil so long for a grave?

III.

His babe grew a man, and still, and still,
 Each night in the window my lamp I trim;
I cannot rest when the winds are shrill,
 Though I know it is I that must go to him!

Oh, the weary nights, and the lagging years!

    Waiting, and watching the treacherous wave;

The heart that is broken can shed no tears,

    And why must we toil so long for a grave?

IV.

I dreamed—I dreamed for years and years,

    My darling came in the night to me,

(Ere waiting had frozen the fount of tears):

    But now such visions can no more be,

For the weary nights, and the lagging years,

    Have withered and changed my heart to stone

And I only dream of the bliss of tears,

    And moan for the tenderness past and gone!

V.

But I see sometimes, when the gloamin' dies,

   (And I hail the sight as a blessèd sign),

A snow-white ship in the far-off skies,

   And a signal comes from his heart to mine!

And the weary nights, and the lagging years,

   Will soon be past—will soon be past!

And God will restore me my smiles and tears,

   And give me my darling at last! at last!

IN MEMORIAM.

GARIBALDI.

(Born, July 22nd, 1807. Died, June 2nd, 1882.)

Amid the people's tears, and love, and wonder—

    Great heart! now all divine—

Amid the drooping flags, and cannon's thunder,

    Permit this waif of mine!

True heart and high! through all thy years of glory,

    Through all life's heavy round,

Never was fairer record, grander story,

    With purer virtue crowned.

Through the long pilgrimage of toil and sorrow,

    Allotted thee of God;

From darkest storm-clad night, to dazzling morrow,

    How nobly thou hast trod!

Calm in the darkness, prudent when earth's highest

    Were kneeling at thy feet;

The People's tears—shed o'er thee as thou liest

    In silence—are most meet!

For thou hast toiled and bled, and given thy treasure—

    Of love, and grief, and pain—

To one grand purpose, without stint or measure—

    To break the tyrant's chain!

And it is done ! where'er thy name is spoken,

    The tyrant cowers in fear ;

And all earth round, this day is shown love's token

    By trembling lip and tear.

It hath been said, count no man safe from falling,

    Until life's storm is past ;

But thy bright star grew brighter to the dawning—

    Undimmed from first to last !

Sleep well !—sleep safe !—time cannot mar thy story

    Through all the coming years ;

Be thine the spotless fame, the crown of glory !

    Be ours the love and tears !

THE DROWNED MAIDEN.

THE storm had ceased, and as the sun uprose,

   We found her sleeping on the cold white sands;

Upon her breast now hushed in calm repose,

   Were clasped, as if in prayer, her small white hands.

We knew not whence she came. Perchance that night

   A ship had foundered, and of all she bore,

Of age, and youth, and manhood in his might,

   Only that maiden frail had reached the shore.

THE DROWNED MAIDEN.

She lay as if in calm, untroubled sleep,
    Pure as a flower of summer, and as fair;
And seaweed from the caverns of the deep,
    Twined 'mid the tresses of her golden hair.

And flowers that bloom far down beneath the deep,
    Circled her brow, and in the morning's breath,
Waved o'er her forehead with a gentle sweep;
    A strange wild wreath that had been wove by death.

There calm and beautiful, at peace she lay,
    With angels watching o'er her rest the while;
And ever o'er her lips there seemed to play,
    Faintly and soft, the shadow of a smile.

Ye who have loved her, weep for her no more.

   Death is an angel unto such as she;

Calmly she slumbers on our lonely shore,

   Hushed by the music of the great sad sea.

GIVE BACK.

Give back, give back! the years within thy keeping,

 Oh, cruel tyrant, Time!

Give back, give back! lost childhood's laughing, weeping,

 That are no longer mine.

Give back, give back! the perfect love I cherished

 That earth is dead without!

Give back, give back! the simple faith that perished

 In the vain sea of doubt.

GIVE BACK.

Give back, give back! the friends that all have vanished

    In the wild maze of life;

Give back, give back! the peace that erst was banished

    By the false, cruel strife.

Give back, give back! the perfect joy of being!

    The bliss that beauty brings!

The esthetic joy of hearing, breathing, seeing

    All nature's perfect things.

Vain cry, poor heart! the mystic charm once broken—

    We leave the magic shore;

The rubicon once passed, the fiat spoken—

    We can return no more!

THE HOUSE WE BUILD AT LAST.

How small the house we build at last!

How strangely altered is our pride;

One darkened room is all we ask,

No garish light on any side;

One narrow bed for perfect rest,

One bed—there is no other guest!

We build it safe, for use, not show,

(All our vain fancies are out-worn),

The roof is very plain and low,

We have no care for praise or scorn;

We learn such perfect taste at last,

When all our vulgar pride is past!

THE HOUSE WE BUILD AT LAST.

We have no care of those who come,

No fear that they will smile or jest

At our small solitary home,

Or say that this, or that, were best;

For in our city, each and all

Build very quietly and small.

We have no restless love for change,

No wish to climb, no fear to fall;

No craving for the new or strange,

No rude, unseemly haste at all;

We've learned the perfect grace of rest,

We've learned that silence is the best!

The storm may rave, the storm may cease,

Or kingdoms sink, or kingdoms rise;

It never breaks our perfect peace,

Whate'er befalls beneath the skies;

THE HOUSE WE BUILD AT LAST.

Our lowly house, and narrow land,

Are safe from envy's cruel hand.

Ah, yes! the home we build at last,

Is better far than all the rest,

What, though the vanity is past!

What, though we have no pleasant guest!

We have forgotten quite to weep,

And learned to be content with sleep.

"VANITY OF VANITIES."

Oh! how we cling to the weary round,

The weary round of the moon and sun,

To life! and dread the silent swound;

And what is it all, when all is done?

A cloud of tears, a flash of light,

A half-forgotten dream of night!

We toil and build, but never dwell,

We gather gold with weary hands;

With eager eyes we buy and sell,

We grasp beyond at far-off lands;

And all the glittering dust we heap,

We leave for other hands to reap!

"VANITY OF VANITIES."

We dream our dream, our sweet love-dream!

When the morning star hangs low i' th' sky,

While the east is red with a golden gleam,

And the lark sings clear and high;

But ere the dreamer has dreamed his fill,

The lips are cold, and the heart is still!

We climb with wounded hands and feet,

The snow-clad peaks of power and fame,

Scorning the valleys low and sweet,

For the vain pride to see our name

One moment glitter in the sun,

Ere the last flash of day is done!

Oh, vain desires! oh, flying years!

Oh, bleeding hearts, and fleeting breath!

Why are we blinded with sad tears,

In fear and trembling of sweet death!

Better is rest, when all is done,

Than every gift beneath the sun!

AKANBAR

I.

There's an island afar in the crimson west,

Where zephyr breathes low with a rapturous sigh,

An island as fair as the isles of the blest,

In a stormless sea, 'neath a cloudless sky.

A sea-girt isle, a glittering gem,

Set in the ocean's diadem.

Close fringed with palms that softly sweep

Their drooping fronds upon the deep,

And drape with grateful shade the sand,

Where laughing children hand in hand

Once spent the long soft tropic day,

On those bright waves, in happy play;

Nor dreamt that ever change could blight

Such lives as theirs, or scenes so bright.

Oh, cruel fate! oh, evil chance!

Why did your blighting foot advance!

To change and mar a scene so fair,

With desolation and despair!

Oh! white-winged peace, in thy sweet name

What deeds of wrong—what deeds of shame—

Are done! and yet the seas of tears

Flow on unhealed through all the years.

II.

Blue are the skies o'er Akanbar,

And soft the light of moon and star;

Sweet isle with charms not found elsewhere,

Matchless in all that's bright and fair.

Like that lone flower of gorgeous hue,

On Java's mountains only found,

Which never greeted human view

Elsewhere on all earth's varied round!

So lies that isle—and never yet

Were scenes of equal beauty met;

Such flashing streams, and gleaming bowers,

Such falling lights, and wealth of flowers,

Such sparkling seas, where clear and bright,

The coral flashes back the light,

Commingled with a thousand dyes,

Of gorgeous colours rippling through

The glancing waves, which mock the skies,

In their bright sheen of limpid blue.

III.

The day-dawn streamed across the bay,

In fiery flash of tropic day ;

And from the groves of living green—

That shone in sparkling silver sheen—

Came wild birds' songs in softest swells,

Like tinkling chimes of fairy bells ;

In such sweet harmony of tone

As ne'er to human skill was known.

No ripples o'er the waters break—

That glitter like a silver lake—

While odours float from wondrous bowers,

Where bloom those strange and magic flowers,

Whose breath makes each and all forget

The past—however prized and dear !—

And ne'er was mortal able yet

To break the spell that chains him here.

When once the magic charm is spread,

The memory of the past is dead;

And the sweet present fills the breast

With full content of perfect rest.

And love—such as the heart when dulled

By fashion, neither knows nor feels,

When those sweet blossoms once are culled,

Like their own odour—softly steals

O'er soul and sense; and nevermore

The past can wake the dreaming ear,

For always on that charmèd shore,

The lotus blooms from year to year.

IV.

List! to Awaiya as she dips

Her flashing paddle in the sea,

And gaily sings, with rosy lips,

A song of island minstrelsy.

Never, I ween, a fairer grace

Was seen on maiden form or face;

And never yet a truer heart

Beat in accord with love and truth,—

A heart adorned with nature's art,

And all the simple grace of youth.

Oh! maiden of the southern seas,

With eyes like thine own wondrous night;

With all the perfect grace of ease,

With step and motion firm, yet light;

In spite of all the studied grace,

Of fashion's slaves, in court or hall,

In rest or motion, form or face,

Love crowns thee, maiden, queen of all!

V.

AWAIYA'S SONG.

1.

The songs of the birds at the dawning of day,

When dewdrops are glancing on thicket and spray,

Fall softly and sweet on the listening ear,

Now faintly and far, and now thrillingly near!

But sweeter than wild bird's most exquisite strain,

Are the whispers of love, when they plead not in vain.

2.

The surf on the reef—when the winds are asleep,

And no breath stirs the palm-trees, or ruffles the deep,

When the voice of the sea, as it rises and falls,

Sweeps landward, and Echo low answering calls

To the heart of the sea—'neath the bright morning star—

Is sweet, but love's whispers are sweeter by far!

3.

The low mountain wind, in the soft twilight hours—
Deep laden with odours of forests of flowers,
As it whispers through groves where the orange-tree
    blows,
And gathers each moment more wealth as it goes—
Is dear to each sense, but far dearer than this,
Are the whispers of love with its passion of bliss!

VI.

The white sails drooped against the mast,
The perfumed zephyr from the shore,
Laden with spice, is floating past,
The last bright gleam of day is o'er.
The rustling leaves begin to play,
After the sleep of tropic day;

The trailing vines, their lustrous flowers

Fling open to night's charmèd hours:

And stars—with one swift flash of light—

Proclaim the presence of the night.

VII.

No tongue can tell how bright it seems—

To weary storm-tossed sailor's eyes—

When first the tropic island gleams,

A perfect earthly paradise!

With all its bowers of bliss and rest

In all their gorgeous colours dressed.

Soft purple peaks—with clouds like snow—

That guard those fairy vales below,

Where silvery torrents gleam and flash,

And down deep shadowy ravines dash,

So sheer that ere they reach the shore

The streams return to mist once more,

Changing to wondrous shapes that rise

In rainbow clouds to meet the skies.

VIII.

The banner of the patient Christ

Waves high o'er lovely Akanbar;

But hearts are dark and eyes are moist,

With hate and fear (as captives' are,

Who see, alas! when all too late,

Their cherished land laid desolate,

By art and cunning and deceit,

And not by open fair defeat).

Proud hearts and hands beneath the guise

Of lowly mien and gentle speech,

With cunning learned 'neath colder skies,

And ready lips, their craft to teach;

Have taught the children of the sun

Instead of love, a desperate hate,

For all the train of evils done,

And seen, alas! when all too late.

Power gained by seeming lack of power,

Pride hidden by the bended knee;

Deeds darker than the darkest hour

That ever gloomed o'er Sunda's sea.

The gentle teaching of the Cross,

Taught—falsely taught—in word, not deed!

Life's purest aims, accounted dross,

And ruined hopes, and hearts that bleed,

Accounted holy! Outward show,

Trampling the simple virtues low;

Oppression's grasping, galling hand,

A darkening cloud o'er all the land;

A baleful, blighting, evil star,

Glares lurid over Akanbar!

IX.

Oh! Spain—once mother of the brave,

Yet cold and cruel as the grave;

No spot of earth hath felt thy power,

But mourns in hate the hapless hour,

Which sent thy soldier-priests to tell

That heaven lay through the gates of hell!

A tale thy ruins prove a lie!

Crumbling to dust 'neath every sky!

X.

Awaiya stands, where high and steep,

The sullen cliff hangs o'er the deep;

Where like a dream, o'er cape and bay,

The golden sunset fades away;

Where far below, the laughing waves

Shimmer and leap through sapphire caves,—

She stands, one rigid arm outspread,

An invocation to the dead.

With face where hatred flashes through,

Can this, can this be she we knew,

With wondrous liquid love-lit eyes,

Like stars in midnight tropic skies;

Can this fierce woman be the maid

Who sang love's whispers half afraid—

With love's delicious wayward fear—

Her song might reach her lover's ear?

XI.

AWAIYA'S DIRGE.

1.

All! all whom I love have departed to sleep.
Then why should I linger to suffer and weep?
To the gods of my people I leave my redress,
All powerful to bane, though unable to bless;
May the curse of my nation still follow the race!
Who have night in their hearts and the dawn on their face.

2.

Farewell to the land where my fathers have bled,
Farewell to the hearts that are broken or dead,
Farewell to the shore where I thought in my bliss,
"Oh, where could a heaven be fairer than this!"

Farewell to the bowers where the voice of the dove

Mingled low with the trembling whispers of love!

3.

I go to the heart that is waiting for me,

Waiting lonely beside the impassable sea;

Who is weary with watching the pathway of light

For the spirit that only can bring him delight;

I come, love! I come where death never can steal

One throb of the bliss we for ever shall feel!

XII.

That isle is still a dream of bliss,

And he who haply wanders there,

Muses, "Can dreamland equal this,

Can heaven excel a scene so fair?"

Still through the sapphire-tinted waves,

Gleam rosy lights from coral caves;

And softly o'er the laughing deep

The rustling palm-fronds lightly sweep.

Still from the purple mountain gleams

The rainbow light of flashing streams.

Still from the groves the wild bird's song

Tells its love story all day long.

And still from day-dawn till nightfall

The tropic sun gleams over all.

And when the soft day yields to night,

The stars shine over bowers so fair,

It seems that never sorrow's blight

Could ere have cast one shadow there !

XIII.

But they who once within those bowers,

With light hearts chased the flying hours ;

Who passed with laughter and delights

Their cloudless days and balmy nights;

Whose hearts a thousand tropic years

Had filled with laughter, not with tears!

Have withered with a dark despair

Their sunny nature could not bear,—

Have drooped beneath the iron rod

Of those who dared to teach that God

Could smile on creeds so dark and stern,

His simple children scorned to learn!

IN THE GULF OF DULCÉ.

It was in the Gulf of Dulcé, in the Port of Isabel,

Ah, Lord! how the moonlight glistened, and the long sharp shadows fell;

How the ocean danced and shimmered like a sea of molten gold,

How the trailers swung, and blossoms hung, can ne'er be sung or told.

'Twas the little schooner *Seahawk* came a-creeping round the head,

With her long low hull and raking spars, and snowy wings outspread;

Came a-creeping through the moonlight (as the heavy tropic breath
Half filled her sails with balmy gales) as silently as death.

We mounted one long carronade on the saucy little craft—
A heavy gun for such a one—with a sixteen-pounder aft;
The carronade for chasing, and the little after-gun
For a shot when men had done their best, but had to cut and run.

Ah! the merry days in Dulcé, moored among the fairy keys,
Or slipping like a sea-gull o'er the wondrous coral seas!

Over gardens spread beneath us, fit for fairy king and queen,
Where coral glanced, and seaweed danced, and fishes slid between.

My true love dwelt in Dulcé, and the Spaniards never guessed
That her sweet lips saved their little town from falling like the rest;
I could let the proud Dons air their pride, their vain bravado take
With a merry quip and laughing lip, for Margarita's sake.

The Lord does all things kind and good, but the Devil mars the same!
His hand was in the hapless work, there was no one else to blame;

He sent the cursèd Spaniards to our bower beside the sea,

Where the fireflies burned their fairy lamps to light my love and me.

The fight was like a tropic storm—fierce, mad, and quickly past,

Wild as the rush o'er summer seas, of the equinoctial blast.

Of those who fell, what recks to tell? Revenged, I ween, they were,

For ten proud Spaniards bit the dust for every "Sea-hawk" there!

I fought hard pressed against a tree, while the blows fell thick and fast,

I was blind with blood, my arm grew weak, and I thought my day was past!

The dead lay high in a wall around, and still they pressed me sore,
When a light form sprang between our swords, and I swooned and knew no more.

A sword flashed through her gentle breast! And then the rescue came!—
They told me after—I did not hear her dear lips breathe my name!
They thought me dead, and they bore me back to a sailor's grave in th' sea,
But they laid her low in mother earth, where a maiden loves to be.

My brave men cried, "Oh, let us back! oh, let us back this day!
And we'll teach the cruel Spaniards how English lads repay;

We'll leave a tale in Dulcé that forgotten ne'er shall be
While sea-gulls fly beneath the sky and fishes swim in sea!"

"Nay, lads! I spared Port Isabel for one I'll no more see,
And for her sake, who loved me so, 'twill never fall by me!
What matter that the Spanish dogs should vaunt, the *Seahawk* fled?
The word I pledged my living love I'll keep though she is dead!"

We sailed away from Dulcé, straight before the soft land breeze,
We crossed the bar as the morning star rose out o' the eastern seas;

We shaped our course for Martinique, and ere that day grew dim,

The purple peaks sank faint and far beneath the ocean's rim.

I looked no more on Dulcé, or the Port of Isabel,

Where the silver moonlight glistened and the long sharp shadows fell;

But I see in dreams, where the firefly gleams, and a great céiba tree,

Where the trailers swung, and blossoms hung, and my true love died for me!

THE DYING BUSHRANGER.

I AM dying, Ben, winged by the bobby!

I knew that long Snider would tell;

But how nicely you gave him his gobby—

How neatly you brought down the swell!

There's a comfort—yes, Ben, a great comfort—

To feel as my checks are sent o'er,

That the cove with the stripes and the breeches,

Sent his in a minute before!

And 'tis doubly sweet to my feelings

That you brought the gum-sucker down;

You were always so just in your dealings—

Oh, Lord! how they'll miss him in town

There are many sweet gals will be piping

Their eyes for the bobby who sleeps,

(Never thinking of love or of fighting),

Far away where the Bayungun sweeps.

Good-bye, Ben! The minutes are flying,

And I have not many to spare;

Don't fear, I'm not snivelling or crying;

But, Ben, just you bury me there,

Where the river winds round by the crossing,

And the red early sun dyes the grass,

Where the wattles their tassels are tossing,

And their scent loads the air as you pass!

That's a spot, Ben, we've camped on so often,

In days when existence was bliss;

When Australia's fierce sunlight would soften

Into nights sweet and balmy as this;

While you and I puffed our tobacco,

Sipping tea from our old blackened can,

And slept—oh, such sleep!—in our 'possums,

And feared neither devil nor man.

And then the long stretches we'd cover

Ere the red dawn had burst into day;

You, Ben, on the black we called "Plover,"

And I on "War-eagle" the grey;

No post-and-rail e'er stayed our going,

No creek was too broad or too deep,

While with hearts and blood bounding and glowing,

Our nags flew like birds at the leap!

THE DYING BUSHRANGER.

Ah, those days! Talk of danger! why, danger

Was a jest, and all life was a joy!

We ne'er hurt a friend, and a stranger

Why, we've helped many new chums, my boy!

We lived at the cost of the stations—

Who ne'er felt the loss of a sheep,

And could well keep us poor coves in rations—

The excitement was worth all our keep.

Do you mind when we stuck up rich Russell,

And had them all tied in a row,

And then all at once had a tussle,

Just when we were ready to go?

When the bobbies rode up and alighted—

There were six, and the sergeant made seven—

It was rude, Ben, to come uninvited!

Three bolted, and four went to heaven.

Do you mind when we found the two children

Away out the Emu Creek way—

Where the wattles in millions had blossomed,

And the plains with scrub-blossoms were gay?

Do you mind how the two little duffers

Were sleeping with never a fear,

As sweetly as angels—or swaggers

On wages and grub by the year?

Do you mind how you carried the girl

In your arms, and I carried the boy,

For fifty long miles to Jack Dawson's,

And the mother half frantic with joy?

Do you mind how she kissed us at parting!

And Jack like a baby would cry?

And the kids—Why, old man, I am starting

For—Your hand, Ben, old chum—and—good-bye!

THE AFGHAN'S VERSION OF THE CAMPAIGN,

1840—1842.

I.

My curse on the pale, greedy race from the west!

The ruthless invaders who never can rest,

Whose instincts of conquest and greed never sleep,—

The race that are careless, who perish or weep;

Who come with a promise to cherish and save,

And end but in giving the conquered a grave!

II.

We gathered from far, by high beacon and flame,

From father, and mother, and lover we came!

From hearths which we knew some would never more
  see,
To rescue our land, or to die with the free!
To drive the proud foe from the sweep of our sky,
Or die as all Afghans are ready to die!

III.

We came from the desert, the shadowy land,
Away o'er the long rolling waste of the sand;
The ghost-haunted desert, the tenantless! where
No sound ever floats on the motionless air!
Save when the wild rush of the deadly simoom
In a moment sweeps rider and steed to their doom.

IV.

We came from the hills that are leafless and bare,
Where the sun-smitten rocks in their nakedness glare;

We came from the peaks that are mantled with snow,

That gleam like the clouds o'er the ravines below;

We came from the vales where the almond-trees wave;

With swords that were keen, and with hearts that were brave.

V.

We came with our souls and our bosoms on fire!

Our hands nerved with hate so they never could tire;

We came in the day, and we came in the night;

Our lances were sharp, and our daggers were bright;

We came to the revel where blood only flows,

To wash our good swords in the hearts of our foes!

VI.

They fell like the leaves when the summer is past,

When swept by the rush of the hurricane blast;

Their white bones are bleaching on desert and hill,

A warning before, and a monument still

Of how we can strike for the freedom we prize,

And the land that we guard as the light of our eyes!

VII.

Beware, oh invader! our ravines are deep,

Our deserts are wide, and our mountains are steep;

Our hands and our swords are the same as before,

And the hate in our hearts is the hatred of yore;

And your blood the white bones of your fathers will stain,

If ye come in the pride of your conquest again!

ISLES OF THE BLEST.

There's an island that men have sought from of old,
    And it lies in a sapphire sea;
Its shores are of pearls, its mountains of gold,
    Immortal fruits hang on each tree;
The mystical lotus is wondrous fair,
    And the nightingales never are mute,
And mingle their song in the slumberous air,
    With the notes of love's magical lute.

Brave voyagers seek for this wonderful isle,
　Nor think they can miss it or fail;
All start on the quest with a confident smile,
　Boldly hoisting a snow-white sail;
Each chooses a pilot to guide him aright,
　Through the beautiful sapphire main;
So sail they away in the golden light,
　But they never come back again.

So sail they away, but they never come back,
　Or they come back weary and worn;
Broken and crushed with the hurricane wrack,
　With sere sails shattered and torn;
None ever moor by the island of gold,
　Though it shines to each like a star;
They hear but the echo of things untold,
　And the nightingales singing afar.

They breathe but the magical odours that blow,

    From the lotus so wondrous fair ;

And 'tis many a year ere the voyagers know

    Their ships cannot carry them there ;

For the island is guarded by spell and bar,

    And the voyagers all grow old,

So they hear not the nightingales singing afar,

    And they see not the mountains of gold.

At last, at last their high hopes fail,

    And their hearts grow weary with pain ;

Their toil-worn hands cannot trim the sail

    They have trimmed so long in vain ;

And the golden peaks that touch the sky,

    And the shadows that sleep between—

Where the fountain of youth and the lotus lie—

    Grow dark, and are no more seen.

THERE IS A ROAD THAT WE MUST TREAD.

THERE is a road that we must tread—

A silent road that mortals fear—

When those we love shall whisper—" Dead !"

And moan to ears that will not hear ;

With all our vain self-flattery gone,

Naked, in silence, and alone !

A strange sad road, from which no breath

Of faintest knowledge—glimmering light—

Hath come since first the spectre death

Led his pale hosts by day and night,

A road o'er which the high and low,

Must in the self-same footsteps go.

A road on which no travellers meet,

No greetings pass of smiles or sighs;

A road where are no weary feet,

But steadfast faces, changeless eyes;

And lips immovable and white!

And brows on which there is no light!

A road where all things mortals prize,

And seek with eager toil and strife—

(The pomp which dazzles human eyes,

All vanity and lust of life,

The wildest dreams of gathered gold)—

Are left by hands grown strangely cold.

A road to which all footsteps go,

All faces turn, all pulses beat,

All mortals hasten fast or slow

With lingering or impatient feet;

And leads the wisest—and untaught—

Beyond the bounds of human thought!

THE SHIPS.

The ships sail out, and the ships sail in,

Unfolding and folding their great white sails;

These weary and eager the haven to win,

Those all-impatient to face the gales;

Some sailing away to the fairy isles,

Some sailing away to the hurricane wrack;

All sped on their way with tears and smiles.

But which will founder! and which come back!

THE SHIPS.

The ships sail in, and the ships sail out,

To the fate that is waiting by day and night;

Though men are fearless, and ships are stout,

Though hearts are merry, and eyes are bright,

They cannot pass where the Shadow stands,

They cannot pass, though stout and brave;

When the place is reached, they fold their hands,

And stay where the Shadow has made their grave.

The ships sail out, and the ships sail in,

Passing, repassing with out-spread wings;

The anchor is tripped with a merry din,

While the careless sailor a roundelay sings;

Some to arrive at the far-off shore,

Where love is waiting with hope and dread;

Some to cast anchor, no more—no more—

No more, till the sea gives up its dead!

The ships sail in, and the ships sail out,

And the days go stretching away to the years;

And men are hemmed by fate about,

We smile our smiles, and weep our tears;

The ship-boy croons some sweet love song,

Thinking the while of his mother's face!

And the ship we thought so brave and strong,

Goes down in the night and leaves no trace!

LINES UPON HEARING A BLIND GIRL PLAY "HOME, SWEET HOME."

"Home, sweet home"! I think the tears and story,
    To your dark eyes convey
Some wondrous visions of a land of glory,
    Where first will dawn your day!

Where the first knowledge of the lights and shadows
    The Master's hand hath wrought;
Where the first lessons on the golden meadows
    Will first to you be taught.

I think it brings to you some deeper meaning,
　　Than our dull sense can feel;
Though outward dark, I think within is gleaming,
　　What words cannot reveal—

Of wondrous lands, beyond time's narrow portal,
　　Where you will first behold,
All! all! earth's fairest things become immortal
　　Upon the streets of gold!

Where the sweet sunshine glorified will glimmer
　　Through groves of endless bliss;
Where the soft light on seraph's wings will shimmer
　　Colours ne'er seen in this.

Where you will first perceive love's outward glory;

In full perfection trace

(Without one spoken word) love's perfect story,

Writ on our Father's face!

And then, ah then! methinks the exaltation

To you will be the more;

Because will burst the wondrous revelation,

Where no light was before.

THE DYING CHIEF.

A DIRGE.

(Translated from the Maori.)

I.

HERE let me die! where I hear the unchanging voice of the ocean,

Here let me die! where I know the wild bird is building her nest;

Here let me die! where the wind keeps the tinkling leaflets in motion,

Here let my spirit depart, and the hands that are weary find rest.

II.

I am old, and the dreams of my youth are scattered like
 autumn leaves falling;
I am old, and the friendships and loves that were mine
 in the far-away past,
Are gone to the land of the dead, away beyond power of
 recalling,
But now the long journey is o'er, and I hear the old
 voices at last.

III.

I hear the sweet voices of friends, such friends as would
 die for a brother,
Such friends as we had in the past, who would die by a
 comrade in fight;

Such friends as we had long ago—as true as the love of a mother;

How cold all the world has grown since they went to the regions of night!

IV.

I hear the soft voice of my love like the music of waters a-falling,

Like the ripple of song when the dawn is breaking o'er forest and hill;

Through all the long shadow of years, I know the sweet words she is calling;

I know the love-light in her eyes is beaming to welcome me still.

V.

Lay me to rest on the hills—where no mortal will trouble my sleeping,

Where the foot of the foe of my race will never come near to my bed;

My hate and my scorn of that race in my sorrowful heart I am keeping,

And will whisper it back in the night, from the undying place of the dead.

VI.

They came with a lie in their hearts, while they spake but of love and forgiving,

They came with the greed of their race, and spake of a brother and friend;

They told of a mystical life, of the sweetness of beautiful
living;
They told us their lives were a truth, the liars! and
this is the end!

VII.

Hush! let me hear once again the whispers from valley
and mountain.
The last lingering note of the bird, ere he wings to his
mate and his nest;
The echo and moan of the sea, the swell of the down-
rushing fountain;
And now let my weary heart sleep, oh! come blessèd
spirit of rest!

THE SADDEST THING.

WHAT is the saddest thing on all the earth,

Over all sorrows, far too deep for tears;

Sadder than death (sweet death our second birth),

The grief of griefs, in our three score of years?

The sorrow, that when e'er its shadows fall,

Hope leaves our threshold never to return;

And thence and always gloom is over all,

However bright our household fires may burn?

THE SADDEST THING.

'Tis not the grave, however dark and deep,

'Tis not the weary feet in far-off lands;

'Tis not the midnight shades, who wake and weep,

With veilèd faces and with outstretched hands.

Over the deepest grave some flowers will bloom,

The tirèd feet some day, some day! will rest;

And the dark shadows in our silent room

Are touched sometimes with light, and rainbow dressed.

'Tis when the heart has left the land of dreams,

And when for us there is no unknown shore;

'Tis when we learn hope is not what it seems,

And light or shade can never touch us more!

'Tis when we learn time's magic healeth all,

And when we know the end of tears and mirth;

When o'er our dreams, life's gloom and knowledge fall,

This is the saddest thing on all the earth!

OH, TRAVELLER OUT IN THE NIGHT.

Oh, traveller out in the night—

In dread and fear—

The dawn of the wonderful light

Is near!—is near!

The terror that fills your heart,

Will soon be past;

The shadow you dread will depart,

At last!—at last!

The sorrow, and hate, and pain,

    Will cease, will cease;

And will come no more again;

    All peace!—sweet peace!

The dreams we dreamed in youth—

    Both I and you—

Of love, and beauty, and truth,

    Are true!—all true!

Oh, traveller out in the night—

    In dread and fear—

The dawn of the wonderful light

    Is near—is near!

So near that we sometimes see—

When stars are bright—

Far over life's sombre sea,

The first faint light

Of the city that needs no sun !—

Oh, hush, poor heart !—

Patience till night is done,

And fear depart !

Patience—each weary year,

Still faster flies ;

Patience ! our sin and fear ;

Our tears, and cries—

Are known to one who stands,
    (Our own sweet Lord!)
With outstretched wounded hands,
    With gracious word;

Waiting to clasp our hands,
    Waiting to bless,
To guide to the nightless lands
    From this!—from this!

Oh, traveller out in the night—
    In dread and fear—
The dawn of the wonderful light
    Is near!—is near!

"AS MANY AS I LOVE, I REBUKE AND CHASTEN."

I.

All precious things do grow from tribulation,
    And each sweet germ must start,
Nourished by tears of blood and desolation—
    Wrung from some sore-tried heart.

II.

All gems of thought that have come down the ages,
    Were wrought from some dark mine,
By the grief-stricken hearts of saints and sages,
    Who made them mine and thine!

III.

Through the dark midnight, toiling, weeping, learning,

    The lesson God must teach;

Ere the true wisdom—ere love's mighty yearning—

    Will touch with fire the speech—

IV.

Will touch with fire the lips, so that in speaking,

    The prophet may reveal

The hidden things that God in love is keeping,

    Things that we dimly feel

V.

Around us as we journey, but for sorrow

    We cannot see aright;

God's wise ones speak, and lo! the golden morrow,

    Breaks on our raptured sight!

TREASURES OF THE DEEP.

FAR in the secret bosom of the deep,

On coral beds, and caves, and glittering sand,

Lie what the ocean evermore will keep,—

The treasures ta'en from many a different land.

There lies the gold from Afric's burning clime,

There lies the wealth of India's gorgeous shore,

There lies the gem from the Peruvian mine,

Hid from the eye of man for evermore.

There lie the implements, once used by man,

To rob his fellow-man of fleeting breath!

The sword now rusted that with blood once ran,

The deep hoarse cannon that rejoiced in death.

There lies the ship that sank amid the fight,

Proudly defiant, with her colours true,

And through her torn sails the pale green light

Falls on the cold white faces of her crew.

There foemen lie—to battle nevermore—

Grasping the useless sword and silent gun;

Their hopes and joys, their fears and anguish o'er!

Their wild, mad, short career of glory done!

There lies the sailor, who from kindred dear—

With no soft hand to soothe his aching head—

Died on the ocean, and o'er whom no tear

Fell, as he wended to his cold sea bed.

There lies the wanderer, who had journeyed far,

Seeking for rest, till hope grew cold and dim;

At length returning to his one true star,

Sank, while the eyes were bright that watched for him.

And there the maiden, draped with golden hair,

(Far from the tender one who gave her birth)

In the sea-grottoes—bright, and calm and fair—

Lies on the sea flowers—a fair flower of earth!

There lies the child of many tears and prayers,

Clasped to its mother's cold unbeating heart,

Ta'en from the world and all life's weary cares,

Saved from the fight ere called to take its part.

No tongue can tell the treasures of the deep,

For man's proud foot may never journey there;

We know a part of what its caverns keep;

Those we have loved, the good! the true, the fair!

We know a part, but man can never tell

All which the ocean evermore will keep;

All that lies hidden 'neath the ocean's swell,

The mourned, the loved, lost treasures of the deep!

A FRAGMENT.

I come from wastes of burning sands;

From dreary steppes of frozen lands;

From isles of palm in summer seas,

From mountain peaks that kiss the breeze;

From moonlit rivers, Indian bowers,

With all their endless wealth of flowers.

I know where the Arab rears his tent;

Where the silent Indian bow is bent;

Where the treacherous Afghan hides i' the grass,

Watching for blood in the narrow pass,

Silent and cruel, and sure as fate,

Ne'er striking too soon, nor waiting too late.

A FRAGMENT.

I know where the desert Bedouins dwell,

Shielded and hidden and guarded well,

By the pathless leagues around them spread,

By the silent caravans of the dead!

Well I know where their oases gleam

With palms and roses and flashing stream.

I know where the Gaucho on matchless steed,

Sweeps over the pampas with lightning speed;

The endless pampas that fall and rise,

Bounded afar by the arching skies :

The ghostly lands, full of charm and spell,

I know their secret, and love them well.

Oh, weary city! oh, weary life!

Toiling and cruel, and full of strife ;

A FRAGMENT.

Endless passing of tirèd feet,

Up and down on the restless street;

Oh for the desert, and oh for the sea!

And oh for the life that is wild and free!

A VOICE FROM THE SEA.

A VOICE came up from the moaning sea,

Over the cold grey waste of sand;

I knew it was coming to me, to me!

And I could not fly, for a cold white hand

Held me like fate, and my heart with fear

Stood still that the message I should hear.

" Dreamer, oh, dreamer! no more, no more,

The crimson dawn in the east appears;

The light that lightened the magic shore

Is dim with the dimness of unshed tears;

And the waves that once were all purple light,

Are weird and dark with the coming night.

"Your ship, oh, dreamer! with silken sails,

That gaily steered from the harbour bar;

Was broken and shattered in midnight gales,

In a silent sea, 'neath the northern star;

And lies like a ghost on a desolate shore,

And will come no more, will come no more!

"On the sunless coast of that silent sea,

(That was never swept by a sea-bird's wing),

Your ship, oh, dreamer! once fair to see,

And freighted with love in the winsome spring!

Lies grim and stark, and her sere, thin sails

Will swell no more to the summer gales.

"No eyes to brighten—no voices to cheer,

No nightingales piping their evening lute;

Only the sand-dunes silent and drear,

Only the ship like a ghost, death mute;

With crumbling decks, and with bleaching spars,

That silently point to the pitiless stars.

"Only the out-stretched claspèd hands,

The shadowy faces, pale, pale, and cold,

You watched and waved from the sloping sands

(Waved with a smile in the days of old),

Only the wailing the memory hears,

When the stars have set on all smiles and tears.

"And now, oh, dreamer! your dreams are past;

The watching is over, the tears are shed;

The slanting shadows are falling fast,

The future is narrow, the past is dead;

Stretch not vain hands o'er the sundering sea,

For the dreams—lost dreams! that no more can be!"

BROTHERHOOD.

"No heart that breathes but learned to weep,
  Ere doubtfully it learned to smile;
And never mortal soul could keep
  Its earthly course, nor mourn the while.

"Thou mayst have joy—thou shalt have woe.
  The sun may shine—the night must fall;
Mirth's careless songs some hearts may know,
  But sorrow's notes are known to all."

THERE is no bond in laughter; grief not gladness,

  Wakes love death only parts;

And the great brotherhood of mortal sadness,

  Unites all human hearts!

BROTHERHOOD.

Who hath not wept ! who hath not met with sorrow,

    Toiling on earth's rude ways !

Who hath not dreamt of sunshine on the morrow,

    And woke to darkened days !

Who hath not moaned for rest, while only seeing

    The desert's endless gloom !

Who hath not seen some heavenly phantom fleeing !

    Who hath not built a tomb !

All hearts on earth have some sad secret keeping,

    Sits by all hearths a ghost ;

Within all households, desolate Rachel weeping,

    Wails for her children lost.

If ye would wake all hearts—touch what is lying
In every human breast;
Speak of the moan of birth, the wail of dying,
And life will teach the rest!

There is no bond in laughter; grief not gladness,
Wakes love death only parts;
And the great brotherhood of mortal sadness,
Unites all human hearts!

THE BURIAL OF THE EARL.

From the halls that his ancestors founded of yore,

From the door that shall open to greet him no more,

From the room where he first saw the day—and where
    last

The Shadow shut out the sweet light as it passed—

My lord cometh forth very grandly and slow,

On the journey all mortals are fated to go.

Throw back the dark gates—bow respectfully low—

Let the solemn hearse pass with its trappings of woe—

Uncover all heads—while in silence and pride

The stately old earl takes his very last ride,

With four noble horses, that seem quite aware

'Tis a branch of Plantagenet glory they bear.

Pass on very slowly in duteous fear,

My lord—is my lord in his house—on his bier!

Pass up the long walk to the mortuary gate

Where the surpliced priests in all reverence wait;

Bear him in—with the deep voices praying before—

Where my lord in his splendour shall enter no more.

Then the low-muttered prayer in the shadowy aisle,

A sob from a woman—a man's careless smile!

And then—dust to dust!—and we all turn again

To the present, of passion—of pleasure—of pain—

To the storm of the city—the calm of the park—

And leave the dead earl alone in the dark!

THE CONFESSION.

I.

SISTER, come nearer! let me feel
Thy soft hand o'er my forehead steal,
That I may know 'tis thou art near,
And that my heart hath naught to fear.
The cold, stern priest I dread to meet,
And though oft kneeling at his feet,
I never yet had power to tell,
What made me seek this lonely cell,
And pass my years of youthful bloom,
Within this fearful living tomb!
Oft to confess at vesper hour
I came, but never had the power.

The cold, hard look, the words that fell

Upon my senses like a knell,

Chilled my heart and bound my tongue,

And though remorse my bosom wrung,

I dared not speak where none would be

To breathe one word of sympathy.

II.

But now when earth and sea are dreaming,

And through the grated window high,

The light of stars is softly streaming,

Like angel glances, from the sky.

To thee, with none save us awake,

My last confession I will make;

My last! for ere to-morrow's sun,

My sands of life will all be run.

III.

'Tis long, and yet not many years!

(For time is measured by our tears)

Since last I saw the roses blow,

Where winding Arno's waters flow.

Since last I listened to the song

Of birds that sang all summer long;

Since last I trained the orange-flower

To shed its perfume o'er my bower.

It seemeth long since that glad time;

And grief hath blighted me and mine!

That bower is gone, the roses dead,

The wild bird from the grove has fled;

Silence and sadness reigneth there;

Where once was joy, is now despair!

That spot with all its beauty gone,

Is like my bosom cold and lone,

A wreck of things that were before,

Young dreams now dead for evermore.

IV.

Sister! didst ever feel the spell

Of love steal o'er thy charmèd heart;

When first the trembling accents fell

So wildly sweet, they made you start?

Ah! if thou hast not, thou wilt deem

My tale is but an idle dream;

A wild, weak fancy of the brain,

I should have crushed, nor thought again.

Oh, sister! by yon glorious star,

That shineth through my window bar;

By my withered, broken heart!

And by the hopes the saints impart!

By all the sorrows I have known,

By penance done with stifled moan !

And by this night, on earth my last,

By all the rapture of the past !

By all fair things beneath the sun,

I'd bear the sorrows of the doomed,

To live one day, as I have done,

On Arno's banks—when roses bloomed !

V.

We grew from childhood, he and I ;

I never was with care oppressed,

Or drew one passing childish sigh,

But it was breathed upon his breast.

We never had a joy apart,

And at the twilight hour, so fair !

We knelt together, heart to heart,

And breathed to heaven our vesper prayer.

And so our childhood passed away
A long and cloudless summer day.

My Adrian grew to manhood, I
The star that ruled his destiny;

While he was all the world to me,
Without whose smile I could not be.

Oh! if such love is wrong in heaven,
I dare not hope to be forgiven;

For I have cherished all the past,
And cannot from my bosom cast

The memory of that early dream,
That happy time when life did seem

The day-dawn of a life of bliss,
The childhood of eternal love,

Whose early years we spent in this,
And perfected in worlds above!

VI.

We parted—why! I need not tell,

I think that all true souls must part;

That bitter parting rang the knell

Of all the bliss love's dreams impart.

Oh! through the weary waste of years

I've known since then, that last farewell

Comes back with all its scorching tears,

That seared my young heart as they fell.

I see him cull the orange-flower—

Bending with perfume, passing fair!—

I see him, as I did that hour,

Place the dear gem within my hair!

I feel him take my death-cold hand,

I see his dark eye fixed on mine,

I see him in his beauty stand,

I hear his voice as plain as thine!

Oh, Mary, mother! spare thy child,

Reason will flee my tortured brain;

Oh! bend on me thy blue eyes mild,

Oh! calm my throbbing heart again!

VII.

Time passed away, I learned to live,

And bear my silent hopeless care;

Life had no more to take or give,

I lived in calm and mute despair;

None knew my sorrow; some there were

Who thought me happy, for they deemed

None smile who have a secret care,

That light from dark hearts never beamed.

They little knew, when smiles are brightest,

And when all inward care seems lost,

And when the laugh and jest are lightest,

The maddened heart endures the most!

As hidden fires are fiercer far,

Than those which cast their flames around;

As streams that for a time you bar,

Will burst their banks and tear the ground!

VIII.

I thought my bitter cup was filled,

I thought that I could bear no more;

I thought that all earth's pangs had thrilled

And seared my life-strings to the core.

But fate had yet a heavier load;

They bade me take—oh, God! oh, God!

I cannot speak it, but 'twas gold,

And high degree and lineage old,

That weighed with them; but when they spoke,

And asked my hand, my passion woke.

Sister, thou knowest I'm mild of mood,

And insult, wrong, and scorn have stood;

But when they mocked my broken heart

With such an insult, there arose

Within my breast with sudden start,

The wild fierce wrath the maniac knows!

They quailed beneath my frenzied eye;

Perchance some pity for my woe

Had touched a chord of sympathy;

I asked not, heeded not to know.

Whate'er the cause, they bade me say

If I would be the bride of heaven,

Or give my broken heart away.

Ah, vain request! the heart is given

Once, only once! and never more

Can be recalled; we ne'er can feel

The rapture we have known before,

When first love's visions o'er us steal;

When the glad earth, so fair and bright,

Seems part of heaven, and angel's eyes

Are gazing on us all the night

From the wide-spreading tender skies;

Smiling to see our charmèd hearts—

Though born of earth so like their own—

This is the glory love imparts,

The spell of bliss, once only known!

IX.

Thou knowest my choice; I bade farewell

To the bright sky and waving flowers;

And lived within this lonely cell,

My only friends---departed hours!

The years went round, yet brought to me

No change, save when the summer came,

For then the little golden bee

Would flutter round my window-pane.

I could not hear their joyous song,

(No sound can pierce that massive wall),

But yet I watched them all day long,

From sunrise until even-fall.

They always came; I think they knew

They brought some happiness to me,

And that the sad hours swifter flew

Gazing on them so glad and free.

I think they mourned that I should be

(When flowers were laden with perfume,

And earth and sky were fair to see),

Not dead, and yet within the tomb!

X.

Sister, farewell! my hour has come,

Ere the moon sets I shall be free!

My weary course on earth is done;

Death brings no pang, save leaving thee—

THE CONFESSION.

Come nearer, for mine eyes are dim—

Still nearer—sister, lay on mine

Thy gentle hand, and sing the hymn

We used to sing at vesper time.

The hymn that tells that we shall meet,

The loved and lost, beyond the tomb;

Where lovely flowers of odours sweet,

Shall through all time for ever bloom.

Where broken hearts shall mourn no more;

Where love shall banish every sigh;

Where the bright dreams we dreamt before,

Shall all be real and never die!

XI.

And this is death! and yet no stings

Wring from my dying lips a moan;

I hear the sound of angels' wings,

Coming to bear my spirit home.

THE CONFESSION.

I hear thy voice, and yet it seems

Like distant echoes, faint and low;

Or some dear voice we hear in dreams,

That soundeth strangely—yet we know

'Tis one for which we moaned and wept

Through midnight hours, with bitter tears;

Whose memory in our hearts we've kept

Through many long and changing years.

And now I hear thy voice no more—

Such heavenly sounds around me swell—

My foot is on the deathless shore—

And he is there! farewell! farewell!

"THE BURDEN OF THE DESERT OF THE SEA."

(A FRAGMENT.)

From an ocean of storm-wrack and terror,

I came to a desolate shore;

Where the mirage spread out like a mirror,

And showed all its ghastliness more;

Not a sound broke the stillness that brooded

O'er the sand-dunes that slumbered like graves,

Save the pain-haunted cry of the plover,

And the moan of the desolate waves.

Sun-scorched, stretched the desert before me,

Unshaded, and barren, and bare;

And the horror of silence was o'er me,

And a shadow I knew was despair;

The sun smote me daily with madness,

And I hated the moon's yellow light,

For her silence, and coldness, and sadness,

Through the ghost-haunted hours of the night.

In the ravines that wound from the ocean,

To the peaks that stood silent as death,

Not a voice stirred the dead air to motion,

Not a sound! not a whisper or breath!

No murmur of insect or fountain,

No sound from the fierce rocks and caves;

Save the echo that moaned from the mountain

Far back to the desolate waves.

I wandered as those that are dreaming,

Who are crushed by unbearable things;

And around me a horror was streaming

Of forms, and the moving of wings;

And of faces and hands that in motion,

Were full of unspeakable dread!

And through all wailed the voice of the ocean,

Far back to the wail of the dead.

I wandered for years! and the blinding

Of sorrow ne'er fell from mine eyes;

I wandered still hopeless of finding

One rift in the fierce brazen skies;

I wandered as those who are seeking,

Surcease from the pain that doth close

The white lips from moaning or speaking,

In the swound of earth's uttermost woes.

With hands and feet wounded and bleeding,

With heart dark as nethermost night,

With the shadow of hope still receding,

I groped for one faint ray of light;

From the peaks where the dead clouds were trailing,

I gazed o'er the limitless sea,

And I knew ships with white wings were sailing—

Fair ships! but they came not to me.

Still on o'er the desert far-reaching,

I journeyed through uncounted years;

Where the white bones of pilgrims were bleaching—

White bones, done with laughter and tears!

I journeyed in search of the sisters,

Sweet sleep—and the sweeter one death;

And though ofttimes I heard their low whispers,

I felt not their lips or their breath!

DESERT OF THE SEA."

Oh, sleep! kin of death, thou art fairer

Than all other gifts that we crave!

Sweet sleep with thy pale sister sharer

Of our homage from cradle to grave;

Ah me! how I moaned for your greeting,

For the touch of your cool loving hands,

For your beautiful forms still retreating

Afar o'er the terrible sands.

THE SPECTRE HORSEMAN.

We were two hunters, we had turned

Our faces from the homes of men,

Our household fires for years had burned

In many a lonely forest glen;

By many a whispering mountain rill,

By many a lake, bright, calm, and still.

It matters not to tell thee why

We lived alone and by the chase;

Suffice it that we had no tie

To bind us to the human race;

Our friendship and our rifles were
The only things that claimed our care.

And ours was not the lukewarm thing
Which men call friendship,—it was truth!
It changed not with time's changing wing,
'Twas not the quick fierce flame of youth;
We made no vows, each other knew,
Whate'er befell, our hearts were true.

It was a glorious summer night,
The silent prairie lay around;
The sky was clear, the stars were bright,
Upon the wind there was no sound,
Save ever as the rustling trees,
Whispered their welcome to the breeze.

We lay in silent dreamy mood,

Beside our camp fire burning low;

Our horses by the chaparral stood;

I watched the shadows come and go;

At length the silence Howard broke,

And glancing o'er the prairie, spoke.

"On such a night the Indians say,

The Spectre Horseman oft is seen;

I wish the ghost would come this way,

I'd ride a race with him, I ween!

My wild, half-broken desert steed

Would try the phantom's boasted speed.

"Besides, he carries double weight;

She, whom the Spanish wretch betrayed,

Though dead, still clings to him in hate,—
The poor, too-trusting Indian maid;
I would I saw the spectre now,
I'd ride a race with him I vow!

"The Indians tell, whoever lays
His hand upon the phantom's rein,
The debt of retribution pays,
And breaks the foul and awful chain
That dooms the maiden thus to ride,
His victim by the demon's side."

And so in idleness we wiled
The lagging hours, until the moon
Stood in the zenith, calm and mild,
And told it would be midnight soon;

When low and faint, I knew not where,

I heard a sound steal through the air!

It grew still plainer, and more plain,

Across the rolling prairie-bed;

It seemed like wolves, and then again

A long, true measured horse's tread;

On, on it came, a strange deep sound,

Until it shook the very ground!

And then between us and the skies,

Across the prairie in the west,

We saw a single horseman rise,

His steed's wild mane and arching crest

Against the sky showed clear and plain

A moment, and then sank again.

THE SPECTRE HORSEMAN.

We grasped our rifles, and our breath

Came quick and short, but neither spoke;

Around us all was still as death,

The calm deep silence only broke

By that strange sound that shook the plain,

And thundered through our throbbing brain!

Another moment and the steed

And rider passed our very side;

We challenged! but his headlong speed

He never stayed, nor slacked his stride;

Our horses, mad with rage and fear,

Plunged fiercely as the shade drew near!

"Quick, mount!" cried Howard, "mount and ride!

Mount! mount! and follow on the chase;

It is the spectre and his bride,

I saw the maiden's ghastly face!

That steed must gallop free and light

If he escapes my hand to-night!"

Each with his rifle at his back,

With fearless heart and ready hand,

We followed on the spectre's track,

Across the dim wild silent land;

And ever o'er the prairie's swell

The ghostly horseman rose and fell.

On! on! beneath the calm moonlight,

We rode abreast, my friend and I;

On! on! into the silent night,

Our noble horses seemed to fly;

On! on! and straight before us fled,

The spectre horse—the living dead!

We rode through bright savannahs, where

The earth with flowers was overspread,

And sweetly on the pure night air,

The perfume from their lips was shed;

And on our burning faces there,

The acacia flung its golden hair.

The bison started from his bed;

The stag a moment gazed, and then

Swifter than thought, away he sped;

The bear growled fiercely in his den;

And from their lair—our deadliest foes—

Upon our track the wolves arose.

They leapt like shadows on our trail,

We saw them gathering o'er the plain;

We heard their low, long, fearful wail

Of mingled triumph and of pain;

And by the moon's clear silver light,

We saw their teeth gleam sharp and white.

Still on we sped, we felt no fear,

Fear!—with our pulses all on fire!—

We now had brought the spectre near,

We saw his eye gleam fierce and dire;

We saw him gazing back in dread;

We saw the maiden's drooping head!

We drew still nearer, nearer still,

We almost touched the phantom's rein;

I felt my heart-blood bound and thrill!

A weight seemed pressing on my brain;

That face beneath the cold moonbeams!—

I yet can see it in my dreams!

"Another length, my gallant steed!
Another, and the race is won!
Another, and a holy deed,
My noble prairie-steed, is done!"
So cried brave Howard, bending low
Across his horse's saddle-bow.

I saw the maiden's dark bright eyes
Flash on my comrade's gallant form;
A flash of fire, as when the skies
Are opened by a thunderstorm;
And when the lightning, wild and bright,
Gleams on the ebon brow of night.

Another moment and the rein—
The spectre's rein—my comrade grasped!

A dim low cloud swept o'er the plain;
And when the white soft vapour passed,
With panting steeds and throbbing brain,
We stood alone upon the plain!

The dawn was breaking; one by one
The cold bright stars began to wane;
Far in the eastern sky the sun
Smiled on the bright fair land again;
And so the race was lost and won,
The deed of retribution done!

WHAT IS LIFE?

Oh! life is a curious thing at the best,

And at most a long journey of sorrow and pain;

We have Solons too many I vow and protest!

Who pretend all its mystery to clear and explain.

But alas, and alas! they but show very clear,

They are cheated, or cheating, and hollow all through;

And when we take hold and examine them near,

They're as far from the truth, sir, as I am, or you!

What is life? Saith the scholar—" A chapter of time,
A page in a book without preface or end ;"
Perhaps this is all very grand and sublime,
But yet it is hardly an answer, my friend !

What is life? Saith the poet—"A dark or bright dream
A short day of joy, or a long night of grief ;
Things are not, and cannot be, what they may seem,
This only is certain, we fade like the leaf ! "

What is life? Saith the priest—" It is made up of prayer,
And list'ning to me, and with texts being crammed ;
Of all other creeds, by St. Thomas, beware !
If you don't follow mine, you are sure to be damned ! "

What is life? Saith the soldier—"A great field of battle,

Where we must for ever beat down or be beaten;

Men are but a purified species of cattle,

And the law of creation is, eat, or be eaten."

What is life? Saith the king—" It is this, to be ruled

By one sceptred head, be he knave, man, or ass;

To be prompt with your taxes, and easily schooled,

And kneel low in the dirt, and stay there till I pass."

What is life? Saith the coward—" 'Tis trembling and weeping,

A long dreary path that but leads to the grave;

A strange, fearful power all our destinies keeping,

Our life but a bubble on time's mighty wave."

What is life? Saith the hero—" A time for the soul
To expand to an angel, great, holy, sublime!
To help, not retard—the stupendous grand whole;
And with fire write our name on the records of time!"

What is life? Saith the maiden—"A day without clouds,
A time to be loved, holy, passionate, true!"
Sweet dreamer beware, there are traitors and shrouds,
And a spectre you see not is waiting for you!

What is life? Saith the youth (with his eye flashing clear)—
" 'Tis a time when all great inspirations have birth;"
Poor boy! ere you're fifty you'll say with a sneer,
That a dinner transcends all the poetry on earth!

What is life? Saith the muckrake—" A time to get gold,

To take care of one's self, never mind who may fall;

Wealth makes a man noble, belovèd, and bold;

There are angels and devils, but gold rules them all!"

What is life? Saith the liar—"A tissue of lies,

Which the fool cannot see, but the knowing can read,

A thousand blanks drawn for one that's a prize!"

Poor scoffer! the devil invented that creed!

What is life? Saith the fool—" 'Tis a queer kind of jest,

A thing to be laughed at, and borne as we can;

The whole is a cheat we must own at the best,

And a worm on a dunghill is perishing man!"

Thus souls yield their fruit! Be that fruit sweet or sour,

It cannot be altered by you or by me;

But the stars are not slain by the cloud of an hour,

Nor do the poor fishes control the great sea!

THE DIFFERENCE BETWEEN A WISE MAN AND A FOOL.

THE one for ever tires his weary brain

With thought by day and night; the other never;

The one goes on in doubt, and dread, and pain;

The other smoothly, as a placid river!

The one toils on up mountains high and steep;

The other takes the easy footpath under;

The one has troubled dreams and restless sleep;

The other snores although all hell should thunder.

THE DIFFERENCE BETWEEN

The one has hollow cheeks and sunken eyes;

The other rosy lips and merry glances;

The one has few bright smiles and many sighs;

The other sings and laughs, and jests, and dances.

The one grasps phantoms, shadowy, wild, and fleet;

The other gold—bright gold! a solid treasure;

The shadows bring the one no solace sweet;

The gold brings many friends, and boundless pleasure.

The one walks barefoot all his life on thorns

The other casts aside as he advances;

The one,—rest, gain, or high position scorns!

The other never loses such good chances.

The one dies young in years, but old in care,

The other groweth old unchanged in feature :

And after death, the one is called a bear !

The other, a most noble, worthy creature !

YARROW BRAES.

O YARROW braes! at last, at last!

I trace with eyes half-blind with tears,

The sunlight o'er thy daisies cast,

Where linger shades of vanished years.

The deathless bards have sung thy praise,

Immortalized in tender song,

Thy bosky dells and sunny braes,

Where sings the lark all summer long.

And I can but in accents tame,

In feeble and imperfect lays,

Whisper the music of thy name—

Thy sweet, sad name—O Yarrow braes!

O Yarrow braes, fair Yarrow braes!

Thy gentle witchery holdeth me

With the sweet charm of olden days,

The wondrous spell o' glamourie!

The magic spell of many a strain

Of sad wild Border ballad lore,

Of tender love, of fierce disdain,

Of daring deeds in days of yore.

Here sleeps, who sang—the saddest wail
That ere was sung on sea or land—
For her dead love in Yarrow vale,
The gallant lord o' Henderland.

And there lies mould'ring Dryhope Tower,
Wrapt in a spell of pensive sorrow,
Where bloomed the peerless Border flower,
The fairest flower on braes o' Yarrow!

And yonder glides the Douglas Burn,
Where Margaret held her lover's rein,
On that sad-fated summer morn,
When all her dark-browed kin were slain.

While the clear burns in chorus chime,

By fell, and scaur, and dingle narrow,

In low soft melancholy rhyme,

The sad sweet " Dowie Dens o' Yarrow."

From every hillside, every glen,

Whisper old tales of love and sorrow,

Of stately dames, and fearless men,

Who lived, and loved, and died on Yarrow.

O Yarrow braes! farewell! farewell!

To me through all the coming years,

Thou shalt be one long magic spell,

Of love, of glamour, and of tears.

THE HEATHER.

I.

Oh, the heather! the bonnie brown heather,
That covered the hills with purple and gold;
Shadow and light of the scented heather,
As the white mist gathered up fold on fold.

II.

Oh, the heather! the sweet brown heather,
Where I met my love by the witches' burn;
Oh, the charm of the golden heather,
The charm that will never again return.

III.

I stand on the hills 'mid the dark brown heather,

The hills that once were all purple and gold;

But I see no light on the sombre heather,

No glory and light, as in days of old!

IV.

I see but the long wild waste of heather;

And the lights and shadows are weird and drear;

The witches' burn as it winds through the heather.

Is wailing a name I shall no more hear.

V.

The cold white mist, as it rolls o'er the heather,

Rolls like a shroud, and is sombre and cold;

And never again shall the dark brown heather,

Be purple and gold, as in days of old.

ELLEN O' ANGUS.

Earl Angus wha ruled in the isles afar,

(Oh, bonnie braw ships wi' silken sails),

Had ae daughter, as fair as the evening star ;

(An' the ships cam' in wi' th' south'ron gales.)

A cruel Sea-king, wha saw her face,

(The hawk aye flies at the whitest dove),

A cruel Sea-king withouten grace ;

(But nane can conquer the king o' love !)

ELLEN O' ANGUS.

A cruel Sea-king, he vowed to take

(Oh, dule an' wae! oh, dule an' wae!)

An' sweet young Ellen his leman make;

(Oh, sorrow betide my natal day!)

This cruel Sea-king had routh o' gold,

(Oh, love is warm, but gold is cauld!)

An' Angus was proud, an' poor, an' old;

(May the curse o'ertake the evil Scald!)

"Oh! father, I lo'e young Ethert the fair,"

(The sea is deep by the Mull o' Finn),

"I've lo'ed him lang, I've lo'ed him sair!"

(The floods are deepest that smoothest rin.)

The Sea-king moored his bonnie ships,

(The throstle is singing wi' meikle glee),

An' he kissed fair Ellen's sweet red lips;

(But the hawk an' the dove can no agree.)

"Oh, dinna ye flutter, an' flee, an' hide,"

(Play up, my piper, play loud an' lang),

"For ye must, and ye sall, be the Sea-king's bride!"

(Strike up, my minstrels, a merry sang!)

"To-night, fair king, when the moon is red,"

(Oh, throstle sing low wi' dule an' fear),

"You'll see me lie in my bridal bed"—

(Sing low an' saft that the dead may hear.)

"But first ye maun gang to the loch o' Finn,"

(Oh, bonnie red moon, shine clear an' fair),

"An look at a mermaid that lies therein,

A sweet young mermaid wi' yellow hair."

The Sea-king gaed to the loch o' Finn,

(Oh, throstle, ye sing but a dreary sang),

An' he looked at the mermaid that lay therein;

He looked fu' sad, and he looked fu' lang!

For it wasna a mermaid that lay asleep—

It wasna a mermaid wi' yellow hair!—

But white as the snaw,—lang fathoms deep—

Sweet Ellen o' Angus was lying there!

There's dule an' wae in Angus Ha'—

(Sail out, black ships, wi' your cruel king!)

Whaur comes nae mair her light fit-fa';

(Oh, throstle wha cares to hear ye sing!)

An' gin ye look, in the howe o' the night,

It's no a mermaid wi' yellow hair—

Like a sheen o' the purest saft moonlight—

It's Ellen o' Angus that's sleeping there.

OUR KNIGHT IS DEAD.

Our knight is dead!—the woeful words are sweeping

    From furthest shore to shore—

Gordon is dead!—add not vain cries of weeping—

    Words cannot utter more!

Our knight is dead! we hardly thought him mortal—

    Our fond hearts could not see

What he saw always through Faith's open portal—

    Over time's narrow sea—

OUR KNIGHT IS DEAD.

The hero's crown—the martyr's scroll of glory

    Writ upon flaming page.

Oh! " Slow of heart "—we will not learn the story

    Sent down from age to age :

" Ever earth's best must suffer, toil, and sorrow !—

    Ever our good must die—

In grief, in pain, in anguish, that the morrow

    May dawn with purer sky."

Oh, brothers !—sisters !—with hearts bowed and broken—

    Over our fallen knight

Clasp faithful hands—in silent loving token !

    We read this lesson right,—

Courage beyond all shame—or doubt—or fearing,
    The love that never fails;
The changeless beacon—flaming—flashing—nearing—
    Through all life's bitter gales!

The steadfast purpose—like a deep pure river,
    That blesses as it flows;
The knight's true quest—to shield the weak, and ever
    Relieve earth's weary woes.

Oh, Christ! Thou knowest—if our true knight taken—
    (Though all knights else did fail)
In grief—alone—uncomforted—forsaken—
    Didst find thy long-lost Grail!

We can no more!—words! words! are void of meaning—
　　With such grief overspread!—
Let each heart frame its dirge—hands clasped—eyes streaming—
　　Gordon—our knight—is dead!

THE NIGHTINGALES.

I.

'Twas in our Devon lanes—ah me!—
Our Devon lanes that are so fair,
With far-off glimpses of the sea,
And hawthorns scenting all the air,
I learnt to love the nightingales,
The sweet, sad, tender nightingales!

II.

'Twas long ago—aye, long ago!

And I was young and he was young,

And we were whispering soft and low

Where thick the hawthorn blossoms hung;

While round us sang the nightingales—

The silver-throated nightingales!

III.

'Twas only foolish vows we made,—

Sweet, silly vows, that lad and lass

Have made so often—in the shade

Of hawthorn boughs upon the grass—

Whilst listening to the nightingales,

The passion-hearted nightingales!

IV.

The sun had set, and all the air

Was trembling with the bliss of life ;

A leaf—a wing—moved here and there,

In all the world there was no strife ;

And then o'er all—the nightingales—

O'er all sweet sounds—the nightingales !

V.

I never saw the stars so bright—

I never saw the sky so blue ;

It was not day, it was not night,

But something half between the two ;

And then—ah, then, the nightingales !

I never heard such nightingales !

VI.

The years they come, the years they go;

The strong must work, the weak must weep;

And some find joy, and some find woe;

And some must wake, and some must sleep;

But still through all, the nightingales

Sing just the same—ah, nightingales!

VII.

I wander through the lanes in spring,

When hawthorns shower their blossoms sweet,

And still the same dear voices sing,

Though his true heart has ceased to beat;

But, ah! they know—those nightingales!

They know it all—those nightingales!

VIII.

He sleeps afar in frozen lands,

Beneath the cruel northern skies;

Ah, God! I could not fold his hands,

Nor kiss once more his loving eyes!

And, oh! there are no nightingales

In those dark lands—no nightingales!

IX.

I think (it may be foolish dreams),

But still I think if he did sleep

Where through the lanes the hawthorn gleams,

And I could clasp his grave and weep,

And we could hear the nightingales,

We both could hear the nightingales!--

X.

Ah! then I think this weary pain—

This weary pain would leave my heart,

And I could smile and weep again,

Because we were not far apart,

And listening to the nightingales—

Both listening to the nightingales!

XI.

'Twas in our Devon lanes—ah me!—

Our Devon lanes that are so fair,

With far-off glimpses of the sea,

And hawthorns scenting all the air,

I learnt to love the nightingales,

The sweet, sad, tender nightingales!

www.ingramcontent.com/pod-product-compliance
Lightning Source LLC
Chambersburg PA
CBHW031955230426
43672CB00010B/2162